D0847084

on
paris

Hemingway
on
paris

'on'

'on'
Published by Hesperus Press Limited
28 Mortimer Street, London W1W 7RD
www.hesperuspress.com

First published in *The Toronto Star*, 1922–3
First published by Hesperus Press Limited, 2010
This edition printed 2013

Used with permission of Scribner, a division of Simon & Schuster, Inc.

Designed and typeset by Fraser Muggeridge studio
Printed and bound by CPI Group (UK) Ltd, Croydon, CR0 4YY

ISBN: 978-1-84391-604-8

All rights reserved. This book is sold subject to the condition that it shall
not be resold, lent, hired out or otherwise circulated without the express
prior consent of the publisher.

Contents

On Paris

Living on $1,000 a Year in Paris
The Toronto Star Weekly, 4th February 1922

Paris. – Paris in the winter is rainy, cold, beautiful and cheap. It is also noisy, jostling, crowded and cheap. It is anything you want – and cheap. *not anymore ...*

The dollar, either Canadian or American, is the key to Paris. With the US dollar worth twelve and a half francs and the Canadian dollar quoted at something over eleven francs, it is a very effective key.

At the present rate of exchange, a Canadian with an income of one thousand dollars a year can live comfortably and enjoyably in Paris. If exchange were normal the same Canadian would starve to death. Exchange is a wonderful thing.

Two of us are living in a comfortable hotel in the Rue Jacob. It is just back of the Academy of the Beaux Arts and a few minutes' walk from the Tuileries. Our room costs twelve francs a day for two. It is clean, light, well heated, has hot and cold running water and a bathroom on the same floor. That makes a cost for rent of thirty dollars a month.

Breakfast costs us both two francs and a half. That totals seventy-five francs a month, or about six dollars and three or four cents. At the corner of the Rue Bonaparte and the Rue Jacob there is a splendid restaurant where the prices are à la carte. Soup costs sixty centimes and a fish is 1.20 francs. The meals are roast beef, veal cutlet, lamb, mutton and thick steaks served with potatoes prepared as only the French can cook them. These cost 2.40 francs an order. Brussels sprouts in butter, creamed spinach, beans, sifted peas, and cauliflower vary in price from forty to eighty-five centimes. Salad is sixty centimes. Desserts are seventy-five centimes and sometimes as much as a franc. Red wine is sixty centimes a bottle and beer is forty centimes a glass.

My wife and I have an excellent meal there, equal in cooking and quality of food to the best restaurants in America, for fifty cents apiece. After dinner you can go anywhere on the subway for four cents in American money or take a bus to the farthest part of the city for the same amount. It sounds unbelievable but it is simply a case of prices not having advanced in proportion to the increased value of the dollar.

All of Paris is not so cheap, however, for the big hotels located around the Opera and the Madeleine are more expensive than ever. We ran into two girls from New York the other day in the Luxembourg Gardens. All of us crossed on the same boat, and they had gone to one of the big, highly advertised hotels. Their rooms were costing them sixty francs a day apiece, and other charges in proportion. For two days and three nights at their hotel they received a bill for five hundred francs, or forty-two dollars. They are now located in a hotel on the left bank of the Seine, where five hundred francs will last two weeks instead of two days, and are as comfortable as they were at the tourist hotel.

It is from tourists who stop at the large hotels that reports come that living in Paris is very high. The big hotelkeepers charge all they think the traffic can bear. But there are several hundred small hotels in all parts of Paris where an American or Canadian can live comfortably, eat at attractive restaurants and find amusement for a total expenditure of two and one half to three dollars a day.

Poincaré's Folly
The Toronto Daily Star, 4th February 1922

Paris. – Canadian interest in European politics is as dead as a bucket of ashes. There are plenty of politics in Canada, and the good Canadian is sick of old-world tangles that are merely older and dirtier than the Dominion product. But all people who were in the war are interested in the inside reason for the turn of events that has cost France the sympathy of the world.

When the armistice came, France occupied the strongest moral position any country could hold. People spoke of "The soul of France." France was immaculate. And then came the peace conference of Versailles.

The world condoned the French attitude at the peace conference because the war was so recent and France had suffered so much that it seemed natural for her to make an unjust, conqueror's peace. It was Clemenceau's peace, his last tigerish move, for now Clemenceau is the deadest name in France. But it was an understandable peace, with the war so recent, and a forgivable peace.

Now the Versailles peace is a long time back, the war is over. Germany is making an earnest effort to build up her country to pay the money she owes the Allies and England is trying to help Germany that she may be able to pay. It is to France's interest to see that Germany has a chance to pay, and she must see that the economic recovery of Germany is necessary if Europe is ever to get back to normal. But France keeps an enormous *as it* standing army, rattles the saber against Germany, destroys the *always* effect of the Washington limitation of armament conference by *is* adopting a Prussian attitude about submarines and talks of the next war.

Nobody that had anything to do with this war wants to talk about another war. Least of all should France want there to be a "next war." The French people do not want any war. But, at present, the French people do not happen to be in control of the French government. That is the secret of the whole thing.

The present Chamber of Deputies, which corresponds to the Dominion Parliament, was elected in the year after the war, and the majority is held by the old reactionary party. They believe that they can get all the money they wish out of Germany if they only threaten her enough and cannot see that they will only produce utter bankruptcy and get nothing. They are the ones who want to go on and occupy the Ruhr basin, not realizing that the occupation would cost more money than she could get from the mines. They are too old to learn new things and they no longer represent the people who elected them.

Those old-line politicians were not satisfied with Premier Briand. He was too gentle, and he was fooling with that terrible thing, Russia. So they forced his resignation. Briand was not liberal enough for the Allies and the United States, but that made no difference. He was forced out and Poincaré made premier.

Now Poincaré and the blindest of the reactionaries are in the saddle and riding for all they are worth. But the ride will not be long, and it will be their last ride for a long time. It is the thin majority of the present chamber, coupled with the stupidest of the professional politicians that are giving the world the impression it is getting of France at present. It is a slim majority, and the next election will wipe it out; then France will resume her place as a nation with the good of herself and the world at heart, and cease to be a military power run by an irascible lot of old gentlemen.

For the French people have been thinking and working while their politicians have been talking. If they hadn't been working so hard (unemployment has almost vanished in France) they would have kicked the present Chamber of Deputies out long before this.

Clemenceau Politically Dead
The Toronto Daily Star, 18th February 1922

Paris. – There is nothing deader than a dead tiger and Georges Clemenceau was a very great tiger. Therefore Georges Clemenceau is very dead.

Coming from Canada, where an interview with Clemenceau still makes the front page of the newspapers, it is one of the big surprises to find that the one-time Tiger of France is as dead politically as that ex-president of France who lost his place through falling out of a moving Pullman car in his pajamas. No one quotes Clemenceau, no one in the government asks Clemenceau's opinion, when you say "Clemenceau" people merely smile, and finally M. Clemenceau has been forced to start a small newspaper to get his views before the public at all.

If you want an explanation of the atrophy of Clemenceau as a political figure you can go to two places to get it. You may interview politicians who will talk about Versailles, the reparations question, open diplomacy, Genoa, the Ruhr basin, and the Kemalists. Or you can go to the cafés and get the truth. For no politicians could keep a man out of the public eye if the people wanted him.

In the cafés the Frenchmen have nothing to gain or lose by the things they say, so they consequently say the things that they believe. Of course if they have been sitting in a café too long they sometimes say even more than they believe. But if you catch a Frenchman when he has been in the café just long enough to come to a boil, and before he has begun to boil over and spill on the stove, you will find out what he really thinks of Clemenceau or anything else. And if you catch enough Frenchmen in different parts of France, you will have the national opinion, the real national opinion, not the shadow of the national opinion that is reflected in elections and newspapers.

"The things Clemenceau says have turned sour in the mouths of the people. They do not taste like truth. They may have been true once, but they do not taste true now," one Frenchman told me.

"But has everyone forgotten what he did in the war?" I asked.

"The war is over and he was a very great tiger in the war, but he wanted to go on being a tiger after the war. After the war tigers are a handicap to a country. You need workhorses and mules, maybe, but not tigers. The people are tired of Monsieur Clemenceau, and he will have to wait until he is dead to be a great man again."

That is the result of the talk of many Frenchmen. It does not go into details, nor cite instances, but France wants a new type of

7

statesman and needs him badly. She wants a builder instead of a fighter, a man who will think forward instead of backward, and because there is no fighting to be done, with the callousness of republics, she has dropped Clemenceau. He lived too long after his job was finished, and now, as the Frenchman in the café said, "he must wait until he is dead to be a great man again."

Paris Is Full of Russians
The Toronto Daily Star, 25th February 1922

Paris. – Paris is full of Russians at present. The Russian ex-aristocracy are scattered all over Europe, running restaurants in Rome, tearooms on Capri, working as hotel porters in Nice and Marseilles and as laborers along the Mediterranean shipping centers. But those Russians who managed to bring some money or possessions with them seem to have flocked to Paris.

They are drifting along in Paris in a childish sort of hopefulness that things will be all right, which is quite charming when you first encounter it and rather maddening after a few months. No one knows just how they live except it is by selling off jewels and gold ornaments and family heirlooms that they brought with them to France when they fled before the revolution.

According to the manager of a great jewel house on the Rue de la Paix, pearls have come down in price because of the large numbers of beautiful pearls that have been sold to Parisian jewel buyers by the Russian refugees. It is true that many Russians are living fairly lavishly in Paris on the sale of jewels they have brought with them in their exile.

Just what the Russian colony in Paris will do when all the jewels are sold and all the valuables pawned is somewhat of a question. It is usually impossible for a large body of people to support themselves indefinitely by borrowing money, although a few people enjoy a great success at it for a time. Of course things may change in Russia, something wonderful might happen to aid the Russian

8

colony. There is a café on the Boulevard Montparnasse where a great number of Russians gather every day for this something wonderful to happen and to recall the great old days of the Czar. But there is a great probability that nothing very wonderful nor unexpected will happen and then, eventually, like all the rest of the world, the Russians of Paris may have to go to work. It seems a pity, they are such a charming lot. *how I feel about myself*

Papal Poll: Behind the Scenes
The Toronto Star Weekly, 4th March 1922

Paris. – Once a week Anglo-American newspaper correspondents resident in Paris meet to talk shop. If the world could have a Dictaphone in the room it would have such a backstage view of European politicians, conferences, coronations and world affairs that it would spin very fast for quite a time from the shock.

All week the correspondents have been mailing or cabling dispatches giving the news as they saw it as trained professional observers. For a couple of hours each Wednesday they talk it over as they saw it as human beings watching human beings instead of newspapermen with diplomas.

"They crowned the pope on a plain pine board throne, put together just for that," says one of the men who has spent twenty-one days in Rome covering the death of the pope [Benedict IV] and the coronation of the new pontiff [Pius XI] for one of the big wireservices.

"It reminded me of a fraternity initiation when I saw the throne and watched them getting the scenery out the day before."

"Afterwards Johnson and I" (the name isn't Johnson, but that of a correspondent of one of the great press syndicates) "were talking with Cardinal Gasparri about why they didn't wait for the American cardinals. Johnson was asking him why they hadn't waited.

"'We do things very quickly here,' Gasparri said to Johnson.

9

"'Perhaps you do them a little too quickly for Americans and Canadians, your eminence,' Johnson said to him.

"'We have to be careful about you newspapermen,' the cardinal said to Johnson.

"'Perhaps you wouldn't have to be if you took us more into your confidence, your eminence,' Johnson answered.

"'Who is that funny little fat man?' Gasparri asked one of his attendants.

"'You have a lot of nerve to call me fat, your eminence,' Johnson said."

The dialogue between the Vatican and the press did not appear in any of the news dispatches. Neither did the news dispatches tell of the difficulties the correspondents had to get their news out of Rome.

All cables were sent from the post office, where there were three rooms for newspapermen. In one of those rooms one typewriter was permitted to be used. More than one typewriter was supposed to make too much noise for the Italian correspondents to be able to think. When the Americans and Britons unlimbered Coronas there was a fearful row.

Half the people in the telegraph office were betting on the result of the balloting for the new head of the church, and when an American correspondent would tear through the crowd from the phone to write on a cable blank, he would be hemmed in by excited shouters demanding in German, French and Italian to know his news.

A papal censorship had been established and all cables containing the names of certain cardinals were automatically held up at the sending office. In the end this censorship protected some correspondents who had learned from "absolutely reliable sources" of the election of a certain cardinal who did not become the new pope, and sent cables announcing his election.

Rome was jammed for the coronation of the pope but there were only about fifty newspapermen. This is accounted for by the speed with which the election of a new pope follows the death of the old; there is not time to get men over from abroad to cover the event. Prices were sky high and double and treble rates in force for Americans.

"I found the way to get through the crowds though," an American correspondent said. "The only people in Italy who wear silk hats are diplomats and so I bought a top hat, and whenever I wanted to get through anywhere I put it on, and it worked like a charm."

By dint of top hats, bribes, shoving, proxies, and Italians to translate the Italian newspapers, the correspondents got the news, and sometimes got it on the wire. To read the even paragraphs in the news dispatches, you would have no idea under what conditions they were written.

Wives Buy Clothes for French Husbands
The Toronto Star Weekly, 11th March 1922

Paris. – At last the balloon-shaped, narrow-at-the-bottom trousers of the French workman are explained. People have wondered for years why the French workingman wanted to get himself up in the great billowy trousers that were so tight at the cuffs as to hardly be able to pull over his feet. Now it is out. He doesn't. His wife buys them for him.

Recently at the noon hour in French factories there has been a great trading of clothing by the men. They exchange coats, trousers, hats and shoes. It is a revolt against feminism. For the wife of a French workingman from time immemorial has bought all her husband's clothes, and now the Frenchman is beginning to protest against it.

Two Frenchmen who served in the same regiment together and had not seen each other since the demobilization aired their grievances in a bus the other day when they met.

"Your hair, Henri," said one.

"My wife, old one, she cuts it. But your hair, also? It is not too chic!"

"My wife too. She cuts it also. She says barbers are dirty pigs, but at the finish I must give her the same tip as I would give the barber."

"Ah the hair is a small matter. Regard these shoes."

"My poor old friend! Such shoes. It is incredible."

"It is my wife's system. She goes into the shop and says, 'I want a pair of shoes for mon mari. Not expensive. Mon mari's feet are this much longer than mine, I believe, and about this much wider. That will do nicely. Wrap them up.' Old one, it is terrible!"

"But me also. I am clothed in bargains. What matter if they do not fit? They are bon marché. Still she is a wonderful cook. She is a cook beyond comparison. My old one, it would take one of your understanding to appreciate what a treasure among cooks she is."

"Mine also. A cook beyond all price. A jewel of the first water of cooks. What do clothes matter after all?"

"It is true. Truly it is true! They are a small matter."

So in spite of the trading that has been going on in the factories and sporadic outbreaks of protest, the reign of feminism will probably continue.

Poincaré's Election Promises
The Toronto Daily Star, 11th March 1922

Paris. – No matter what your political views may be, it is impossible not to admire the way ex-President Raymond Poincaré, newly appointed prime minister of France, is administering his government.

M. Poincaré has a difficult task. It was made more difficult because for a long time before he came back into power he had been explaining from the outside just what he would do if he were in power. <u>Then he was suddenly required to do all the things he had been suggesting as an onlooker. The situation presented difficulties.</u>

It is easier to advise than execute and so far M. Poincaré has occupied no territory, nor sent French troops into any new territory. But he and his government have settled down to a study and administration of their various departments that is drawing much admiration. Meetings of the heads of various departments are held each week and the underheads confer constantly. This efficiency contrasts with the Briand government, which was greatly lacking in liaison between its different branches.

Financial affairs look better each day. The inflating of the paper currency has been stopped. Unemployment is daily less and French export trade is booming. Germany's meeting of her indemnity payments in the present revised schedule has been a stabilizing factor.

Of course the French budget is still a long way from balancing, and there are the national defense bonds, which run from three months to a year in length, to be paid. The official journal has recently announced that there will be no more of these bonds issued. That means that those outstanding, some 68 billion francs according to reports, will have to be paid inside of a year at the latest. The government may plan to convert them to long-term bonds, but the people who have bought them have tied up their money with the understanding that they are to get it back in a year. Being French people, there is a very great chance that at the end of the year, the six months or the three months, they will ask for their money in cash. That may start the paper-money presses going again.

Meanwhile the Poincaré ministry is going well. "France was quite sick," an American writer who has lived in France for many years said to me the other day, "and she tried all sorts of medicines. Finally, after she had tried doctors of all sorts, she took to Poincaré, who is a patent medicine." Now it appears that the patent medicine is making a cure.

Sparrow Hat on Paris Boulevards
The Toronto Star Weekly, 18th March 1922

Paris. – Parisian milliners have at last discovered a use for the English sparrow. The sparrow hat has made its appearance on the boulevards and the unpopular little bird has come into its own.

The new hat, of which milliners assure me they are having a big sale, is a brown, mushroom-shaped affair with a girdle of stuffed English sparrows. The sparrows look as though they were nestling against the band of the hat and there are about fifteen of them to a headpiece.

So far the milliners are pushing the sparrow creation strongly. Still, you never can tell, it took monkey fur a long time to catch on but the only thing that will ever end the monkey-fur rule now is for the monkeys to give out. The peculiar long-furred monkey has to be imported from Africa and South America and is becoming noticeably scarcer. There will not be that trouble with sparrows at any rate.

Black Novel a Storm Center
The Toronto Star Weekly, 25th March 1922

Paris. – "Batouala," the novel by René Maran, a Negro, winner of the Goncourt Academy Prize of 5,000 francs for the best novel of the year by a young writer, is still the center of a swirl of condemnation, indignation and praise.

Maran, who was born in Martinique and educated in France, was bitterly attacked in the Chamber of Deputies the other day as a defamer of France, and biter of the hand that fed him. He had been much censured by certain Frenchmen for his indictment of French imperialism in its effects on the natives of the French colonies. Others have rallied to him and asked the politicians to take the novel as a work of art, except for the preface, which is the only bit of propaganda in the book.

Meanwhile, René Maran, black as Sam Langford [the boxer], is ignorant of the storm his book has caused. He is in the French government service in Central Africa, two days' march from Lake Tchad, and seventy days' travel from Paris. There are no telegraphs or cables at his post, and he does not even know his book has won the famous Goncourt Prize.

The preface of the novel describes how peaceful communities of 10,000 blacks in the heart of Africa have been reduced to 1,000 inhabitants under the French rule. It is not pleasant and it gives the facts by a man who has seen them, in a plain, unimpassioned statement.

Launched into the novel itself, the reader gets a picture of a native village seen by the big-whited eyes, felt by the pink palms, and the broad, flat, naked feet of the African native himself. You smell the smells of the village, you eat its food, you see the white man as the black man sees him, and after you have lived in the village you die there. That is all there is to the story, but when you have read it, you have seen Batouala, and that makes it a great novel.

It opens with Batouala, the chief of the village, waking up in his hut, roused by the cold of the early morning and the crumbling of the ground under his body where the ants are tunneling. He blows his dead fire into life and sits, hunched over, warming his chilled body and wondering whether he will go back to sleep or get up.

It closes with Batouala, old and with the stiffened joints of his age, cruelly torn by the leopard that his spear-thrust missed, lying on the earth floor of his hut. The village sorcerer has left him alone, there is a younger chief in the village, and Batouala lies there feverish and thirsty, dying, while his mangy dog licks at his wounds. And while he lies there, you feel the thirst and the fever and the rough, moist tongue of the dog.

There will probably be an English translation shortly. To be translated properly, however, there should be another Negro who has lived a life in the country two days' march

from Lake Tchad and who knows English as René Maran knows
French.

American Bohemians in Paris
The Toronto Star Weekly, 25th March 1922

Paris. – The scum of Greenwich Village, New York, has been
skimmed off and deposited in large ladles on that section of Paris
adjacent to the Café Rotonde. New scum, of course, has risen to
take the place of the old, but the oldest scum, the thickest scum
and the scummiest scum has come across the ocean, somehow,
and with its afternoon and evening levees has made the Rotonde
the leading Latin Quarter showplace for tourists in search of
atmosphere.

It is a strange-acting and strange-looking breed that crowd
the tables of the Café Rotonde. They have all striven so hard for
careless individuality of clothing that they have achieved a sort
of uniformity of eccentricity. A first look into the smoky, high-
ceilinged, table-crammed interior of the Rotonde gives you the
same feeling that hits you as you step into the bird-house at the
zoo. There seems to be a tremendous, raucous, many-pitched
squawking going on, broken up by many waiters who fly around
through the smoke like so many black and white magpies. The
tables are full – they are always full – someone is moved down
and crowded together, something is knocked over, more people
come in at the swinging door and, having shouted your order at
his disappearing back, you look around you at individual people.

You can only see a certain number of individuals at the
Rotonde on one night. When you have reached your quota you
are quite aware that you must go. There is a perfectly definite
moment where you know you have seen enough of the Rotonde's
inmates and must leave. If you want to know how definite it is,
try and eat your way through a jug of soured molasses. To some
people the feeling that you cannot go on will come at the first

16

mouthful. Others are hardier. But there is a limit for all normal people. For the people who crowd together around the tables of the Café Rotonde do something very definite to that premier seat of the emotions, the stomach.

For the first dose of Rotonde individuals you might observe a short, dumpy woman with newly blond hair, cut Old-Dutch-Cleanser fashion, a face like a pink enameled ham and fat fingers that reach out of the long blue silk sleeves of a Chinese-looking smock. She is sitting hunched forward over the table, smoking a cigarette in a two-foot holder, and her flat face is absolutely devoid of any expression.

She is looking flatly at her masterpiece that is hung on the white plaster wall of the café, along with some 3,000 others, as part of the Rotonde's salon for customers only. Her master-piece looks like a red mince pie descending the stairs, and the adoring, though expressionless, painter spends every afternoon and evening seated at the table before it in a devout attitude.

After you have finished looking at the painter and her work you can turn your head a little and see a big, light-haired woman sitting at a table with three young men. The big woman is wearing a picture hat of the "Merry Widow" period and is making jokes and laughing hysterically. The three young men laugh whenever she does. The waiter brings the bill, the big woman pays it, settles her hat on her head with slightly unsteady hands, and she and the three young men go out together. She is laughing again as she goes out of the door. Three years ago she came to Paris with her husband from a little town in Connecticut, where they had lived and he painted with increasing success for ten years. Last year he went back to America alone.

Those are two of the twelve hundred people who jam the Rotonde. You can find anything you are looking for at the Rotonde – except serious artists. The trouble is that people who go on a tour of the Latin Quarter look in at the Rotonde and think they are seeing an assembly of the great artists of Paris. I want to correct that in a very public manner, for the artists of

Paris who are turning out creditable work resent and loathe the Rotonde crowd,

The fact that there are twelve francs for a dollar brought over the Rotonders, along with a good many other people, and if the exchange ever gets back to normal they will all have to go back to America. They are nearly all loafers expending the energy that an artist puts into his creative work in talking about what they are going to do and condemning the work of all artists who have gained any degree of recognition. By talking about art they obtain the same satisfaction that the real artist does in his work. That is very pleasant, of course, but they insist upon posing as artists.

Since the good old days when Charles Baudelaire led a purple lobster on a leash through the same old Latin Quarter, there has not been much good poetry written in cafés. Even then I suspect that Baudelaire parked the lobster with the concierge down on the first floor, put the chloroform bottle corked on the washstand and sweated and carved at the *Fleurs du Mal* alone with his ideas and his paper as all artists have worked before and since. But the gang that congregates at the corner of the Boulevard Raspail have no time to work at anything else; they put in a full day at the Rotonde.

Wild Night Music of Paris
The Toronto Star Weekly, 25th March 1922

Paris. – After the cork has popped on the third bottle and the jazz band has brayed the American suit- and cloak-buyer into such a state of exaltation that he begins to sway slightly with the glory of it all, he is liable to remark thickly and profoundly: "So this is Paris!"

There is some truth in the remark. It is Paris. It is a Paris bounded by the buyer's hotel, the Folies Bergère and the Olympia, traversed by the Grands Boulevards, monumented with

Maxim's and the So-Different, and thickly blotched with the nightlife resorts of Montmartre. It is an artificial and feverish Paris operated at great profit for the entertainment of the buyer and his like who are willing to pay any prices for anything after a few drinks.

The buyer demands "that Paris be a super-Sodom and a grander Gomorrah" and once alcohol loosens his strong racial grasp on his pocketbook he is willing to pay for his ideal. He does pay for it too, for the prices charged at the various Parisian resorts that begin to liven up around midnight are such that only a war profiteer, a Brazilian millionaire, or an American on a spree can pay.

Champagne, that can be bought anywhere in the afternoon for 18 francs a bottle, automatically increases in price after ten o'clock to 85 to 150 francs. Other prices are in proportion. An evening at a fashionable dancing café will cut into a foreigner's pocketbook to the extent of at least 800 francs. If the pleasure-seeker includes a supper in his program he will be lucky to get out without spending a thousand francs. And the people he is with will do it all so gracefully that he will, after the first bottle, consider it a privilege until the next morning when he contemplates the damaged bankroll.

From the taxi-driver who automatically cranks up five francs on his meter as soon as he picks up an American, either North or South, from in front of a fashionable hotel, to the last waiter in the last place he visits who has no change under five francs, the study of rooking the rich foreigner in search of pleasure has been reduced to a fine art. The trouble is that no matter how much he pays for it, the tourist is not seeing what he really wants.

He wants to see the nightlife of Paris and what he does see is a special performance by a number of bored but well-paid people of a drama that has run many thousands of nights and is entitled "Fooling the Tourist." While he is buying champagne and listening to a jazz band, around the corner somewhere there is a little Bal Musette where the apaches, the people he thinks he is seeing, hang out with their girls, sit at long benches in the little smoky room, and dance to the music of a man with an accordion who keeps time with the stamping of his boots.

On gala nights, there is a drummer at the Bal Musette, but the accordion player wears a string of bells around his ankle and these, with the stamping of his boots as he sits swaying on a dais above the dancing floor, give the accent to the rhythm. The people that go to the Bal Musette do not need to have the artificial stimulant of the jazz band to force them to dance. They dance for the fun of it and they occasionally hold someone up for the fun of it, and because it is easy and exciting and pays well. Because they are young and tough and enjoy life, without respecting it, they sometimes hit too hard, or shoot too quick, and then life becomes a very grim matter with an upright machine that casts a thin shadow and is called a guillotine at the end of it.

Occasionally the tourist does come in contact with the real nightlife. Walking down the quiet hill along some lonely street in a champagne haze about two o'clock in the morning, he sees a pair of hard-faced kids come out of an alley. They are nothing like the sleek people he has just left. The two kids look around down the street to see if there is a policeman in sight and then close in on the night-walking tourist. Their closing in and a sudden dreadful jar are all that he remembers.

It is a chop back of the ear with a piece of lead pipe wrapped in [Le] Matin that does the trick and the tourist has at last made contact with the nightlife he has spent so much money in seeking.

"Two hundred francs? The pig!" Jean says in the darkness of the basement lit by the match which Georges struck to look at the contents of the wallet.

"The Red Mill holds him up worse than we did, not so, my old?"

"But yes. And he would have a headache tomorrow morning anyway," says Jean. "Come on back to the Bal."

The Mecca of Fakers
The Toronto Daily Star, 25th March 1922

Paris. – Paris is the Mecca of the bluffers and fakers in every line
of endeavor from music to prizefighting. You find more famous
American dancers who have never been heard of in America;
more renowned Russian dancers who are disclaimed by the
Russians; and more champion prizefighters who were prelimin-
ary boys before they crossed the ocean, per square yard in Paris
than anywhere else in the world.

This state of affairs exists because of the extreme provinciality
of the French people, and because of the gullibility of the French
press. Everyone in Canada knows the names of half a dozen
French soldiers and statesmen, but no one in France could give
you the name of a Canadian general or statesman or tell you who
was the present head of the Canadian government. By no one
I mean none of the ordinary people; shop keepers, hotel owners
and general bourgeois class. For example, my *femme de ménage*
was horrified yesterday when I told her there was a Prohibition
in Canada and the States. "Why have we never heard of it?" she
asked. "Has it just been a law? What then does a man drink?"

An American girl was recently billed at the Paris music halls
as "America's best-known and best-loved dancer." None of the
recent arrivals in Paris from the States had ever heard of her,
but Parisians flocked to see the American "Star." Later it came
out that she had a small part in a U.S. musical show some years
ago.

Russians have inundated the city. They can get away with
almost anything, because it is easy for a Russian to claim that
he was anything he may want to say, in Russia; there is no way
to check up on Russian reputations at present. So we have great
Russian dancers, great Russian pianists, flutists, composers, and
organists – all equally bad.

Jack Clifford, who styled himself the colored light-heavy-
weight champion of the United States and Canada, was a recent

nine-days' wonder in France. He avoided meeting any fighters and demanded tremendous sums to box, but announced his willingness to meet Carpentier if a suitable purse was offered. No American had ever heard of him – but the Europeans swallowed him whole.

Clifford met his downfall in Vienna, where a third-rate Austrian pugilist, with an unpronounceable name, punished him so badly that the fight was halted in the third round to save the Negro from further punishment. Clifford had been on the floor most of the evening and did not show even an amateur's knowledge of fighting. The crowd, which had paid several baskets of kronen apiece to see the American black champion, attempted to lynch Clifford with the ropes cut from the ring, but the Negro was saved by the police and left Vienna that night.

At present a familiar figure to those Torontonians who attend boxing matches is basking in the pleasant spotlight of European publicity. It is none other than Soldier Jones. Jones is being hailed by the Paris papers as "the heavyweight champion of Canada, the man who has never been knocked off his feet, the winner of eighty-five fights by knockouts and the best fighter that Canada has ever produced."

Jones is at present in England, where he is being groomed for a fight with [Joe] Beckett, but his manager has sent press dope over to Paris, where it is being published by the English papers and avidly copied by the French.

Torontonians who recall what happened one night last year, when this same Soldier Jones abandoned caution so far as to enter the ring with Harry Greb, will be able to form their own opinions of how easy it is to become a "champion" abroad. The only rule seems to be that you must choose to be a champion of some very distant country and then stay away from that country. That is the way the fiddlers, fighters, painters and dancers are doing.

M. Deibler, A Much-Feared Man
The Toronto Daily Star, 1st April 1922

Paris. – Monsieur Deibler is the most feared man in France. Deibler lives comfortably and respectively in a snug bourgeois suburb of Paris. He is a large, jovial-looking man and his neighbors know that he has some permanent position or other with the Ministry of Justice. They do not fear Deibler on the Avenue de Versailles, where he lives, because they do not know Deibler.

Every so often Deibler and three heavily built men go off on a mysterious trip. They are accompanied by a boxcar that carries the very grimmest load a French train has ever hauled. It is these trips that have earned Deibler his name of the most feared man in France, for in the boxcar is a guillotine.

Deibler is the permanent public executioner of France. He receives a fixed salary and fees for executions out of which he pays his three husky assistants. One of his assistants is his son-in-law, who, when business is light, runs a small café.

Deibler has two guillotines. One is a very large model, a replica of the grim framework that stood in the Place de la Concorde when the tumbrils jolted along the cobbled, narrow way of the Rue St. Honoré. The large guillotine is used for executions in Paris. The other guillotine is much smaller and is kept loaded in a special box ready to travel with Deibler and his three aides to any part of the provinces.

Under the French law a condemned prisoner is not told the time of his execution until an hour before it is to occur. Execution takes place at day-break. The condemned man is aroused, signs certain papers, is given a cigarette and a drink of rum, the barber is called in to shave the back of the prisoner's neck and he is marched out to meet Monsieur Deibler. The guillotine is set up just outside the prison gate and troops keep any spectators a hundred yards away. It is the French law.

When it is all over, M. Deibler and his three muscular assistants take down the guillotine and go back to Paris, where the son-in-law totals up the receipts of his café and Monsieur Deibler returns to his family. The Avenue de Versailles is glad to see him back, he is a very jolly man, and his neighbors say, "Deibler's back. He's been away on another of his trips for the government. I wonder what this Deibler does, anyway?"

95,000 Wear the Legion of Honor
The Toronto Daily Star, 1st April 1922

Paris. – Have you your cross of the Legion of Honor? If not, there is not much chance of getting it now for the boom days are past.

M. Raynaldy, of the French Chamber of Deputies, threw a handful of sand into the smooth-working distribution of decorations of the Legion of Honor when he placed some figures before a committee that was considering granting a number of honors on the occasion of the Molière tercentenary.

Since the armistice, M. Raynaldy's figures show, 95,000 decorations of the Legion of Honor have been granted. 72,000 of these decorations were exclusively military and 23,000 were awarded to civilians for work during the war. You cannot walk twenty yards on the Grands Boulevards without seeing the familiar red ribbon of the Legion in someone's buttonhole.

After seeing M. Raynaldy's figures, the committee unanimously rejected the proposal to grant any new decorations on the occasion of the Molière festival.

Active French Anti-Alcohol League
The Toronto Daily Star, 8th April 1922

Paris. – Models of ravaged brains and livers, dramatic colored charts, posters showing father brandishing a drink in one hand and a black bottle in the other, while he kicks the children about the house, hold a crowd open-mouthed all day before a great window frontage on the Boulevard St. Germain.

Thirst-driven Americans see the exhibit and shudder. They are afraid it presages the beginning of the end of what they regard as the golden age of European culture; the present blissful time when the French bartender has at last learned to mix a good martini and a palate-soothing bronx. For the big window on the boulevard houses the exhibit of the Ligue Nationale Contre Alcoolisme, a name that needs no translating.

The league is not a prohibition measure. It is, strictly, a league against alcoholism and is receiving the support of a large faction of the French people. Already it is making itself felt in France; its posters are in all railway stations and public places, and its greatest practical achievement has been the banishment of absinthe from France.

Its posters read something like this:
1 – Do you know that liqueurs are one of the greatest causes of tuberculosis?
2 – Do you know that apéritifs are deadly poisons?
3 – Do you know that the use of picons often leads to insanity?

At the bottom of the poster, however, in small type, is the announcement that the league does not want people to drink only water; but no, there are the wines of France, yes, and the beers. It describes some and tells of their good effects so attractively that the reader usually leaves the poster in search of a café. The Frenchman still believes that water is only useful for washing and to flow under bridges.

Just across from the offices of the league is the Deux Magots, one of the most famous of the Latin Quarter cafés. Here at tables you see students sipping the liqueurs that cause tuberculosis, quaffing the apéritifs that are deadly poisons, and swigging the picons that often lead to insanity. But occasionally they cast an eye toward the crowd in front of the league window, and as they walk up the boulevard, they have a worried look at the models that show the horrible state of the human liver and lights under alcohol. The window has a sort of fascination for them.

An educational campaign takes years, but I believe that it is the beginning of the end and that alcohol, except for wine, beer and the cider of the north, is doomed in France. The reason I think so is because of the look on the students' faces when they leave the league's window, the fact that absinthe has already gone, and because the anti-alcohol forces are organized while the consumers are not. It is only a question of time.

Parisian Boorishness
The Toronto Star Weekly, 15th April 1922

Paris. – The days of Alphonse and Gaston are over. French politeness has gone the way of absinthe, pre-war prices and other legendary things. It has become so bad that French newspapers have carried columns of discussion on the question of how the French can regain the position they once held as the politest people in the world.

There is such pushing in the Paris subway, cheating women of their seats in the crowded buses, violent rows over prices, barefaced demands for tips in the once polite city that the person who knew Paris in the days before the war would turn away in horror. It is a very different Paris from the old days when the French people enjoyed a world reputation for pleasant gentleness, affability, and instinctive kind attention.

Cabdrivers, of course, always have been discourteous. They are so because they expect never to see their fares again, in a city of tens of thousands of drifting cabs, and have one object: to see how much they can get out of their trip.

It is a safe generalization that no non-French-speaking person ever paid the fare shown on the cab meter and supplemented it with a ten percent tip without having the cabby follow him into his destination cursing and raving that he has been cheated. It is simply a case of the cabdriver having found that there is as much money in doing that as in driving a cab.

The Paris buses provide the worst instances of the new rudeness. You rise in a bus to offer a lady your seat and a walrus-mustached Frenchman plops into it, leaving you and the lady standing. If you say anything to him, he will roar something like this at you: "Eject me if you dare. Try it! Lay just one finger on me and I will have you before the police!"

As a matter of fact, he is in a strongly entrenched position. No matter what the provocation, a foreigner must keep his temper in France. The French engage in some terrific battles with each other, but they are entirely verbal. Once you put a finger on a man, no matter how aggravating the circumstances, you are guilty of assault and go to jail for a term running upward from six months.

Next to the buses and subways, the minor government officials give the most offense to courtesy. These are the men in parks and museums, not the police; for the police, through the most trying times, have remained courteous, polite and obliging.

For instance, there is the reptile house in the Jardin des Plantes, the great Paris zoological gardens. People were coming out of the door of the reptile house when I went up to it. It was placarded as being open from eleven to three o'clock. It was twelve o'clock when I tried to enter.

"Is the reptile house closed?" I asked.

"Fermé!" the guard said.

"Why is it closed at this hour?" I asked.

"Fermé!" shouted the guard.

"Can you tell me when it will be open?" I queried, still polite. The guard gave me a snarl and said nothing.

"Can you tell me when it will be open?" I asked again.

"What business is that of yours?" said the guard, and slammed the door. Then there is the office where you go to get your passports stamped in order to leave Paris. There is a large sign on the wall saying employees are paid and that it is forbidden to tip them. The visa costs two francs forty centimes. I gave the clerk, back of the long board counter, five francs. He made no move to give me any change and when I stood there he sneered at me and said, "Oh, you want the change, do you?" and slammed it down on the counter angrily.

Those are all samples of the type of thing one encounters daily in Paris. Marcel Boulanger, writing in the *Figaro*, holds out hope for the future.

"But I believe that the soul of good society is still fine enough and at bottom – clear at the bottom, alas – sufficiently gracious," he says, after deploring the present state of politeness in France.

"Three centuries of civilization and of the spirit of the salon are not to be lost in four or five years. Nothing good is done without trouble. Observe the fashion in which, except in the homes of the newly rich, one introduces the son of a celebrity! One never says in a breath, 'Monsieur So and So, son of the illustrious Monsieur So and So,' as if the only reason the son had to exist were to carry the name of his famous father. On the contrary, one shades the introduction in spite of himself: 'Monsieur So and So,' says one. Then, after an instant, and smiling gently: 'Monsieur So and So is the son of the illustrious Monsieur So and So.' Thanks to the pause, the remark takes on the air of a courtesy between you, as if you were congratulating the father on having such a son.

"A thousand precautions of taste still are part of the current conversation and may be reinstated. They form a powerful arm which in ordinary times a man carries against wretchedness."

A Veteran Visits the Old Front
The Toronto Daily Star, 22nd July 1922

Paris. – Don't go back to visit the old front. If you have pictures in your head of something that happened in the night in the mud at Paschendaele or of the first wave working up the slope of Vimy, do not try and go back to verify them. It is no good. The front is as different from the way it used to be as your highly respectable shin, with a thin, white scar on it now, is from the leg that you sat and twisted a tourniquet around while the blood soaked your puttee and trickled into your boot, so that when you got up you limped with a "squidge" on your way to the dressing station.

Go to someone else's front, if you want to. There your imagination will help you out and you may be able to picture the things that happened. But don't go back to your own front, because the change in everything and the supreme, deadly, lonely dullness, the smooth green of the fields that were once torn up with shell holes and slashed with trenches and wire, will combine against you and make you believe that the places and happenings that had been the really great events to you were only fever dreams or lies you had told to yourself. It is like going into the empty gloom of a theater where the charwomen are scrubbing. I know because I have just been back to my own front.

Not only is it battlefields that have changed in quality and feeling and gone back into a green smugness with the shell holes filled up, the trenches filled in, the pillboxes blasted out and smoothed over and the wire all rolled up and rotting in a great heap somewhere. That was to be expected, and it was inevitable that the feelings in the battlefields would change when the dead that made them both holy and real were dug up and reburied in big, orderly cemeteries miles away from where they died. Towns where you were billeted, towns unscarred by war, are the ones where the changes hit you hardest. For there are many little towns that you love, and after all, no one but a staff officer could love a battlefield.

There may be towns back of the old Canadian front, towns with queer Flemish names and narrow, cobbled streets, that have kept their magic. There may be such towns. I have just come from Schio, though. Schio was the finest town I remember in the war, and I wouldn't have recognized it now – and I would give a lot not to have gone.

Schio was one of the finest places on earth. It was a little town in the Trentino under the shoulder of the Alps, and it contained all the good cheer, amusement and relaxation a man could desire. When we used to be in billets there, everyone was perfectly contented and we were always talking about what a wonderful place Schio would be to come and live after the war. I particularly recall a first-class hotel called the Due Spadi, where the food was superb and we used to call the factory where we were billeted the "Schio Country Club."

The other day Schio seemed to have shrunk. I walked up one side of the long, narrow main street looking in shop windows at the fly-speckled shirts, the cheap china dishes, the postcards showing about seven different varieties of a young man and a young girl looking into each other's eyes, the stiff, fly-speckled pastry, the big, round loaves of sour bread. At the end of the street were the mountains, but I had walked over the St. Bernard Pass the week before and the mountains, without snow caps, looked rain-furrowed and dull; not much more than hills. I looked at the mountains a long time, though, and then walked down the other side of the street to the principal bar. It was starting to rain a little and shopkeepers were lowering the shutters in front of their shops.

"The town is changed since the war," I said to the girl, she was red-cheeked and black-haired and discontented-looking, who sat on a stool, knitting behind the zinc-covered bar.

"Yes?" she said without missing a stitch.

"I was here during the war," I ventured.

"So were many others," she said under her breath, bitterly.

"Grazie, Signor," she said with mechanical, insolent courtesy as I paid for the drink and went out.

That was Schio. There was more, the way the Due Spadi had shrunk to a small inn, the factory where we used to be billeted now was humming, with our old entrance bricked up and a flow of black muck polluting the stream where we used to swim. All the kick had gone out of things. Early next morning I left in the rain after a bad night's sleep.

There was a garden in Schio with the wall matted with wisteria where we used to drink beer on hot nights with a bombing moon making all sorts of shadows from the big plane tree that spread above the table. After my walk in the afternoon I knew enough not to try and find that garden. Maybe there never was a garden.

Perhaps there never was any war around Schio at all. I remember lying in the squeaky bed in the hotel and trying to read by an electric light that hung high up from the center of the ceiling and then switching off the light and looking out the window down the road where the arc light was making a dim light through the rain. It was the same road that the battalions marched along through the white dust in 1916. They were the Brigata Ancona, the Brigata Como, the Brigata Tuscana and ten others brought down from the Carso to check the Austrian offensive that was breaking through the mountain wall of the Trentino and beginning to spill down the valleys that led to the Venetian and Lombardy plains. They were good troops in those days and they marched through the dust of the early summer, broke the offensive along the Galio-Asiago-Canoev line, and died in the mountain gullies, in the pine woods on the Trentino slopes, hunting cover on the desolate rocks and pitched out in the soft-melting early summer snow of the Pasubio.

It was the same old road that some of the same old brigades marched along through the dust of June of 1918, being rushed to the Piave to stop another offensive. Their best men were dead on the rocky Carso, in the fighting around Goritzia, on Mount San Gabrielle, on Grappa and in all the places where men died that nobody ever heard about. In 1918 they didn't march with the ardor that they did in 1916, some of the troops strung out so badly that, after the battalion was just a dust cloud way up the road, you would see poor old boys hoofing it along the side of the road to ease their bad feet, sweating along under their packs and rifles and the deadly Italian sun in a long, horrible, never-ending stagger after the battalion.

So we went down to Mestre, that was one of the great railheads for the Piave, traveling first class with an assorted carriageful of evil-smelling Italian profiteers going to Venice for vacations. In Mestre we hired a motorcar to drive out to the Piave and leaned back in the rear seat and studied the map and the country along the long road that is built through the poisonous green Adriatic marshes that flank all the coast near Venice.

Near Porto Grande, in the part of the lower Piave delta where Austrians and Italians attacked and counterattacked waist-deep in the swamp water, our car stopped in a desolate part of the road that ran like a causeway across the green marshy waste. It needed a long, grease-smearing job of adjustment on the gears and while the driver worked, and got a splinter of steel in his finger that my wife [Hadley] dug out with a needle from our rucksack, we baked in the hot sun. Then a wind blew the mist away from the Adriatic and we saw Venice way off across the swamp and the sea standing gray and yellow like a fairy city.

Finally the driver wiped the last of the grease off his hands into his over-luxuriant hair, the gears took hold when he let the clutch in and we went off along the road through the swampy plain. Fossalta, our objective, as I remembered it, was a shelled-to-pieces town that even rats couldn't live in. It had been within trench-mortar range of the Austrian lines for a year and in quiet times the Austrian had blown up anything in it that looked as though it ought to be blown up. During active sessions it had been one of the first footholds the Austrian had gained on the Venice side of the Piave, and one of the last places he was driven out of and hunted down in and very many men had died in its rubble- and debris-strewn streets and been smoked out of its cellars with *flammenwerfers* during the house-to-house work.

We stopped the car in Fossalta and got out to walk. All the shattered, tragic dignity of the wrecked town was gone. In its place was a new, smug, hideous collection of plaster houses, painted bright blues, reds and yellows. I had been in Fossalta perhaps fifty times and I would not have recognized it. The new plaster church was the worst-looking thing. The trees that had been splintered and gashed showed their scars if you looked for them and had a stunted appearance, but you could not have told in passing, unless you had known, how they had been torn. Everything was so abundantly green and prosperous-looking.

I climbed the grassy slope and above the sunken road where the dugouts had been to look at the Piave and looked down an even slope to the blue river. The Piave is as blue as the Danube is brown. Across the river were two new houses where the two rubble heaps had been just inside the Austrian lines.

I tried to find some trace of the old trenches to show my wife, but there was only the smooth green slope. In a thick prickly patch of hedge we found an old rusty piece of shell fragment. From the cast-iron look of the smoothly burst fragment I could tell it was an old bit of gas shell. That was all there was left of the front.

On our way back to the motorcar we talked about how jolly it is that Fossalta is all built up now and how fine it must be for all the families to have their homes back. We said how proud we were of the way the Italians had kept their mouths shut and rebuilt their devastated districts while some other nations were using their destroyed towns as showplaces and reparation appeals. We said all the things of that sort that as decent-thinking people we thought – and then we stopped talking. There was nothing more to say. It was so very sad.

For a reconstructed town is much sadder than a devastated town. The people haven't their homes back. They have new homes. The home they played in as children, the room where they made love with the lamp turned down, the hearth where they sat, the church they were married in, the room where their child died, these rooms are gone. A shattered village in the war always had a dignity, as though it had died for something. It had died for something and something better was to come. It was all part of the great sacrifice. Now there is just the new, ugly futility of it all. Everything is just as it was – except a little worse.

So we walked along the street where I saw my very good friend killed, past the ugly houses toward the motorcar, whose owner would never have had a motorcar if it had not been for the war, and it all seemed a very bad business. I had tried to recreate something for my wife and had failed utterly. The past was as dead as a busted Victrola record. Chasing yesterdays is a bum show – and if you have to prove it, go back to your old front.

Sinclair Lewis's Horsebacking
The Toronto Star Weekly, 5th August 1922

They are telling a story in Paris on Sinclair Lewis, author of *Main Street*, that is unconfirmed by Mr. Lewis, but that has a strange ring of truth about it.

According to the story, Lewis on a recent visit to London, where he was working on a new novel to appear this fall, expressed a desire to ride in Rotten Row. He was astonished at the shortness of the Row and said as much to the groom that was accompanying him.

The groom, who had been eyeing Lewis's seat in a grieved and pained manner for some time, drew himself up in disgust.

"Well, sir," he said very haughtily over the top of his stock, "You cawn't expect the bloomin' prairies 'ere sir."

The Great 'Apéritif' Scandal
The Toronto Star Weekly, 12th August 1922

Paris. – The great "apéritif" scandal that is agitating Paris has struck at the roots of one of the best-loved institutions of France.

Apéritifs, or appetizers, are those tall, bright red or yellow drinks that are poured from two or three bottles by hurried waiters during the hour before lunch and the hour before dinner, when all Paris gathers at the cafés to poison themselves to a cheerful pre-eating glow. The apéritifs are all patented mixtures, contain a high percentage of alcohol and bitters, have a basic taste like a brass doorknob, and go by such names as Amourette, Anis Delloso, Amer Picon, Byrrh, Tomyysette and twenty others. Now apéritifs blossom in Paris as new cigarettes do in Toronto. It is simply a matter of the number of persons anxious to try anything new.

The first scandal came when police discovered that absinthe, which was abolished six years ago, was being sold in great quantities under the name of Anis Delloso. Instead of producing a beautiful green color that minor poets have celebrated to the driest corners of the world, the absinthe manufacturers were turning it out in quantity production as a pale yellow syrup. It had the familiar licorice taste, however, and turned milky when water was added – and it had the slow, culminating wallop that made the boulevardier want to get up and jump on his new straw hat in ecstasy after the third Delloso.

One loud, glad cry was uttered on the boulevards and in a few days word-of-mouth advertising made Anis Delloso the most popular beverage in the city. It continued until the police sup-pressed the manufacture of absinthe.

Anis Delloso is still being manufactured. It still has the licorice flavor – but the boulevardier waits in vain for the feeling that makes him want to shinny rapidly up the side of the Eiffel Tower. For it is not absinthe any more.

Now the big scandal is concerned with the Fourteenth of July. Bastille Day is the great French holiday. This year it started on Wednesday night, the thirteenth of July, and continued unabated all Wednesday night, all day Thursday, all night Thursday, all day Friday, all night Friday, all day Saturday, all night Saturday, all day Sunday, and all night Sunday. All big places of business, all department stores and banks were closed from Wednesday afternoon till noon on Monday. It would take about eight columns of closely set type to do justice in any way to that holiday.

Every two blocks there was a street ball where the people of that quarter danced. The street was decorated with colored lanterns and flags and music furnished by the municipality. That all sounds very tame and quiet, but it was not. Orders were given that neither buses nor taxicabs could go down a street where a ball was in progress. As a result there was no traffic.

The music for the ball in the street below our apartment consisted of an accordion, two drummers, a bagpiper and a cornettist. These four courageous and tireless men sat in a wagon box that was placed on four huge wine casks in the street and bowered with branches broken, I believe, from trees in the park. In this sylvan bower they sat, drank, ate, relayed one another on the instruments and played from 9 o'clock at night until 8 o'clock the next morning, while the crowd polkaed round and round!

This happened on four consecutive nights, while the inhabitants of the quarter had a little sleep in the daytime and the rest of the time jammed the street to dance. It was a wonderful thing to watch between twenty and thirty couples dancing hilariously in the street at eleven o'clock in the morning after having danced all night. These were not students or artists or such crazy people, mind you, but shop girls, butchers, bakers, laborers, tram conductors and laundresses, and bookmakers. It was a very great party – but it couldn't have occurred on water.

Enter the "apéritif" scandal. The government spent some millions of francs on the party. It was all considered wisely spent money in the cause of encouraging patriotism. French flags were everywhere, fireworks went off at all times, there was a great military review at Longchamps at eight o'clock in the morning, attended by thousands of people who had danced all night, and went to sleep on the grass. An unbalanced young Communist took a shot at a prefect of police by mistake for M. Poincaré and the patriotic crowd mobbed him. Everyone agreed that M. Poincaré's life was undoubtedly saved by the Fourteenth of

July because who could be expected to hit anyone they shot at after such a night as all Paris had just spent. It was a fine celebration.

The scandal consisted in the fact that above all the dancing places, over the heads of the musicians, where the government had placed the French flags and spent money for the music and decorations, were enormous banners advertising the different brands of apéritifs. Over the ball, flanked by the tricolor, would be a great sign "Drink Amourette." At another place the people of the quartier would be dancing in an ecstasy of patriotism under the legend "Vive Anis Delloso – the Finest Apéritif in the World."

No one seemed to notice the signs to any great extent during the evenings, but once the dancing was over a big inquiry was ordered to investigate why the government spent over a million francs to give the apéritif manufacturers about a million dollars worth of publicity. Several Paris newspapers have come out against there ever being such a July fourteenth again. There is a fearful scandal on and the inquiry about the apéritif signs still continues.

Rug Vendors in Paris
The Toronto Daily Star, 12th August 1922

Paris. – No one can sit for twenty consecutive minutes in front of any Parisian café without becoming aware, aurally or nasally, of the fur rug vendor. Wearing a dirty red fez, a bundle of skins slung over his shoulder, a red morocco billfold in his hand, his brown face shining, the rug seller is as firm a feature of Paris life as the big green buses that snort and roar past, the little, old, red one-lung taxis that grind and beetle through the traffic or the sleek cat that suns herself in every concierge's window.

The rug seller comes by, smiles at each table, and spreads out one of his handsome fur rugs. If you assume such an expression as might fasten itself on the face of the Hon. Mr. Raney on the occasion of his receiving a delegation of the Young Men's Pari-Mutuel Association with a request for him to contribute some fitting sum toward cushions for the seats at the Woodbine [race-track] and at the same time inform the rug vendor, with a dirty look, that you hate all rugs and have just come out of jail after having served twenty years for killing rug sellers on the slopes of Montparnasse, he may pass on to the next table.

Twenty to one, however, would be a good bet against his doing so. It is much more likely that he will fix you with a sad, brown stare and remark, "Monsieur jests about my beautiful rugs."

Now, if you, at this point, arise and kick the rug vendor with your strongest foot, at the same time hitting him heavily over the head with a café table and cry out in a loud clear voice: "Death to robbers and rug vendors!" there is a small chance that he will perceive that you are not in the market for rugs and move on to the next table. It is much more likely, however, that he will slip to his knees, grasp your foot in one hand, bow his head to the blow of the table and say, in a patient voice: "Monsieur kicks and hits me. It is on account of my beautiful rugs."

There is nothing for you to do after that but help him to his feet and ask: "How much?"

The rug vendor unslings something that looks like a royal Bengal tiger from his shoulder and spreads it out lovingly: "For you, Monsieur, two hundred francs."

You examine the royal Bengal tiger closely and perceive it is a beautifully patched and dyed goat skin.

"It is a goat," you say.

"Ah, no, Monsieur," says the rug vendor sadly. "It is a veritable tiger."

"It is a goat!" you grunt fiercely.

"Ah yes, Monsieur," the rug vendor puts his hand on his heart, "it is a veritable tiger. I swear by Allah."

"It is a goat," you repeat. "Stop this lying."

"Ah yes, Monsieur," the rug vendor bows his head. "It is a veritable goat."

"How much do you charge for this mean, ill-dyed, foul-smelling goat?"

"A gift to you, Monsieur, for one hundred francs."

"Forty francs. The last price," you say grimly.

The rug vendor puts the rug over his back and walks sadly away. "You jest, Monsieur, you jest about the beautiful skins. We cannot trade together."

You go back to your newspaper but in a moment there is a familiar aroma. You raise your eyes and there is the rug vendor. He is holding out the royal Bengal tiger. "A sacrifice. For Monsieur, because of his gentility, this beautiful tiger for fifty francs."

You pretend that the rug vendor is nonexistent. He goes off again but comes back. "Forty-five francs," he says brightly. "For Monsieur alone of all the world. Forty-five francs and Monsieur owns the very beautiful tiger."

"I have bought a thousand like it for forty francs," you answer, turning back to the newspaper.

"It is yours, Monsieur. You have bought it for forty francs. The beautiful tiger."

The beautiful tiger is laid across the back of your chair and at once commences his lifelong job of getting hair on your clothing. You give the rug vendor two twenty-franc notes and he bows low. He goes off a little way but you see him eyeing you. He comes back.

"Perhaps Monsieur would care for one of these lovely morocco pocketbooks," he says, smiling happily.

There is only one thing to do. Leave the café.

Several hundred rug vendors are employed by a syndicate that makes the rugs and pocketbooks and pays the salesmen five francs a day and everything they get over the minimum price. Rugs are usually priced at 200 francs to start, with a minimum price about 45 francs. Most of the salesmen are Arabs.

Many of the rugs are well made and very fine-looking and are good bargains at from 45 to 55 francs. Tourists buy them at

from 75 to 150 francs and are invariably satisfied with them –
unless the goat develops atavistic tendencies in the hot weather.
For that there is no remedy.

Did Poincaré Laugh in Verdun Cemetery?
The Toronto Daily Star, 12th August 1922

Paris. – Did Premier Poincaré really laugh in the cemetery at
Verdun when the United States government decorated the
martyred city?

Whether M. Poincaré laughed or not, the pictures taken of
him at the time caused the French Communist party to launch
a bitter attack on the premier, brought forth a white-hot denial
from M. Poincaré, caused a debate in the Chamber of Deputies,
threw France into an uproar and also resulted in the country
being flooded with postcards.

The picture published with this article was issued by the
French Communist party in the form of a postcard, and
first made its appearance at one of the Sunday Communist
meetings held in the country outside of Paris. It shows M.
Poincaré and United States Ambassador Herrick walking in
the cemetery at Verdun and shows both M. Poincaré and the
ambassador apparently laughing heartily. The Communists,
who had always accused M. Poincaré of a great share in the
responsibility for the war, issued the card with a flamboyant
inscription, calling it "The Man Who Laughs" and saying that
"Poincaré, like other murderers, returns to the scene of his
crimes."

In a short time the Communist headquarters had sold over
100,000 of the postcards. The matter came to a head in the
Chamber of Deputies when a young Communist deputy smiled
at some remark of M. Poincaré's in regard to Communist propaganda in the French colonies in Northern Africa.

"You smile?" said M. Poincaré.

"Yes, I smile," said Vaillant-Coutourier, the young deputy who was one of the great war heroes of France, "but I do not laugh in the cemetery of Verdun!"

M. Poincaré went white with rage, and denounced the postcard as a fake and demanded that the entire matter be cleared up with an interpellation. That is, that the Communists accuse him publicly from the floor, and that he answer.

"I never laughed in the cemetery at Verdun," M. Poincaré said, denying the charge absolutely and categorically. "The explanation of the matter is that the sun got into my eyes and twisted my face so that it looked as though I were laughing."

M. Poincaré has stuck to this explanation through thick and thin.

An interesting Toronto angle to the story appears here in the fact that the *Star* on July 22, in their picture page, published, long before there was any controversy or before the Communists had issued their postcard, a picture of Ambassador Herrick and M. Poincaré, taken at the same ceremony as the picture that has caused the great trouble. The *Star*'s picture shows Ambassador Herrick obviously laughing but whether M. Poincaré is smiling must be left to the judgment of the reader.

According to the French papers, Ambassador Herrick gave two explanations of the affair. The papers first quote him as saying that of course he did not laugh, and after being shown the picture as saying, "Perhaps something I said to M. Poincaré made him laugh."

There are two divergent explanations already. M. Poincaré says he did not laugh. Ambassador Herrick says perhaps something he said to M. Poincaré made him laugh.

Now comes a third explanation. A movie photographer who was present on the occasion says that he was hurrying to get in front of Poincaré and Herrick and was running along with his tripod when he slipped and fell sprawling and both the French premier and the ambassador laughed heartily at his ridiculous plight.

Whatever the explanation, the incident, the debate in the Chamber of Deputies, and the postal card have raised a furor in France. Over 200,000 of the postcards have been sold and they are selling at present at the rate of 15,000 a day. Communists charge that those sent through the mail are being destroyed, but those familiar with the French policy of complete freedom of speech in politics doubt this. At any rate they have made their appearance in England.

"What if M. Poincaré did laugh at the cemetery?" many people will ask. "Anyone might have laughed accidentally. What is all the furor about anyway?"

To understand all that you must realize the French attitude toward the dead. It is safe to say that no living man in France today commands as much respect as any dead man does.

Marshal Foch, Anatole France, Henri Barbusse, M. Poincaré or the Pope could never, any one of them, receive the united respect of all the people they would meet if they drove two blocks down the Champs-Elysées. There are too many people with too many divergent political, religious and ethical views in France for any one person to be a complete national hero. But everyone in a motor bus, regardless of religion or politics, takes off their hats when the bus passes a hearse, even if it is a draggled black hearse with only one mourner walking behind. Even the caps of the motormen and chauffeurs come off when they pass a funeral.

It is that great spirit of respect for the dead, coupled with the significance of Verdun, that has given the question of whether M. Poincaré laughed or not the national prominence it holds.

Homes on the Seine
The Toronto Daily Star, 26th August 1922

Paris. – Instead of driving people back to the land, the Parisian apartment shortage is driving flat-dwellers on to the water.

A socially prominent Parisian, finding his rent tripled on the expiration of his lease, inaugurated the new movement by refusing to sign on at the advanced figure, buying an old canal barge, he remodeled it into a super-comfortable dwelling. The barge is large and roomy, the carpentry cost a fraction of the increased rent demanded, and the barge-dweller has a home he can moor in the Seine in the center of the most fashionable quarter. There are four bedrooms, a drawing room, kitchen, bathroom, dining room and billiard room in the floating flat and the owner is summering in it at present at Strasbourg, having crossed the width of France in a very enjoyable trip through the canal system of the Marne, Meuse and Moselle rivers.

Less pretentious "flat boats" are being launched at regular intervals and there is talk of a firm turning out standardized floating homes at popular prices for those Parisians who are desperate about the housing shortage.

The gravity of the housing situation was shown the other day by a rush on a Paris concierge who advertised a flat for rent through official channels. At nine o'clock in the morning the concierge informed the police that there was a flat vacant in the building at an annual rental of 1,800 francs. By five that afternoon the flat was rented.

In the next morning's official journal appeared the notice that the flat was for rent. By noon nearly four thousand people had gathered to see about the flat. It looked like a riot and the concierge called the police, who dispersed the crowd and helped the concierge letter a big sign announcing that the flat was already rented.

A Paris-to-Strasbourg Flight
The Toronto Daily Star, 9th September 1922

Strasbourg, France. – We were sitting in the cheapest of all the cheap restaurants that cheapen that very cheap and noisy street, the Rue des Petits Champs in Paris.

We were Mrs. [Hadley] Hemingway, William E. Nash, Mr. Nash's little brother, and myself. Mr. Nash announced, somewhere between the lobster and the fried sole, that he was going to Munich the next day and was planning to fly from Paris to Strasbourg. Mrs. Hemingway pondered this until the appearance of the rognons sautés aux champignons, when she asked, "Why don't we ever fly anywhere? Why is everybody else always flying and we always staying home?"

This being one of those questions that cannot be answered by words, I went with Mr. Nash to the office of the Franco-Rumanian Aero Company and bought two tickets, half price for journalists, for 120 francs, good for one flight from Paris to Strasbourg. The trip is ten hours and a half by best express train, and takes two hours and a half by plane.

My natural gloom at the prospect of flying, having flown once, was deepened when I learned that we flew over the Vosges Mountains and would have to be at the office of the company, just off the Avenue de l'Opéra, at five o'clock in the morning. The name Rumanian in the title of the firm was not encouraging, but the clerk behind the counter assured me there were no Rumanian pilots.

At five o'clock the next morning we were at the office. We had to get up at four, pack and dress and wake up the proprietor of the only taxi in the neighborhood by pounding on his door in the dark, to make it. The proprietor augments his income by doubling at nights as an accordion player in a bal musette and it took a stiff pounding to wake him.

While he changed a tire we waited in the street and joked with the boy who runs the charcuterie at the corner and who had gotten up to meet the milkman. The grocery boy made us a couple of sandwiches, told us he had been a pilot during the war, and asked me about the first race at Enghien. The taxi driver asked us into his house to have a drink of coffee, being careful to inquire if we preferred white wine, and with the coffee warming us and munching the pâté sandwiches, we drove in state down the empty, gray, early-morning streets of Paris.

The Nashes were waiting at the office for us, having lugged two heavy suitcases a couple of miles on foot because they did not know any taxi drivers personally. The four of us rode out to Le Bourget, the ugliest ride in Paris, in a big limousine and had some more coffee in a shed there outside the flying field. A Frenchman in an oily jumper took our tickets, tore them in two and told us that we were going in two different planes. Out of the window of the shed we could see them standing, small, silver-painted, taut and shining in the early-morning sun in front of the airdrome. We were the only passengers.

Our suitcase was stowed aboard under a seat beside the pilot's place. We climbed up a couple of steps into a stuffy little cabin and the mechanic handed us some cotton for our ears and locked the door. The pilot climbed into his seat back of the enclosed cockpit where we sat, a mechanic pulled down on the propeller and the engine began to roar. I looked around at the pilot. He was a short little man, his cap backwards on his head, wearing an oil-stained sheepskin coat and big gloves. Then the plane began to move along the ground, bumping like a motor-cycle, and then slowly rose into the air.

We headed almost straight east of Paris, rising in the air as though we were sitting inside a boat that was being lifted by some giant, and the ground began to flatten out beneath us. It looked out into brown squares, yellow squares, green squares and big flat blotches of green where there was a forest. I began to understand cubist painting.

Sometimes we came down quite low and could see bicyclists on the road looking like pennies rolling along a narrow white strip. At other times we would lift up and the whole landscape would contract. Always we were bounded by a smoky purple horizon that made all the earth look flat and uninteresting. And always there was the strong, plugged-out, roaring, the port-holes to look out of, and back of us the open cockpit with the bridge of the pilot's broad nose and his sheepskin coat visible with his dirty glove moving the joystick from side to side or up and down.

We went over great forests, that looked as soft as velvet, passed over Bar le Duc and Nancy, gray red-roofed towns, over St. Mihiel and the front and in an open field I could see the old trenches zigzagging through a field pocked with shell holes. I shouted to Mrs. Hemingway to look out but she didn't seem to hear me. Her chin was sunk forward into the collar of her new fur coat that she had wanted to christen with a plane trip. She was sound asleep. Five o'clock had been too much.

Beyond the old 1918 front we ran into a storm that made the pilot fly close down to the ground and we followed a canal that we could see below us through the rain. Then after a long stretch of flat, dull-looking country we crossed the foothills of the Vosges that seemed to swell up to meet us and moved over the forest-covered mountains that looked as though they rose up and fell away under the plane in the misty rain.

The plane headed high out of the storm into the bright sunlight and we saw the flat, tree-lined, muddy ribbon of the Rhine off on our right. We climbed higher, made a long, left turn and a fine long swoop down that brought our hearts up into our mouths like falling in an elevator and then just as we were above the ground zoomed up again, then settled in another swoop and our wheels touched, bumped, and then we were roaring along the smooth flying field up to the hangar like any motorcycle.

There was a limousine to meet us to take us in to Strasbourg and we went into the passenger shed to wait for the other plane. The man at the bar asked us if we were going to Warsaw. It was all very casual and very pleasant. An annoying smell of castor oil from the engine had been the only drawback. Because the plane was small and fast and because we were flying in the early morning, there had been no airsickness.

"When did you have your last accident?" I asked the man back of the refreshment bar.

"The middle of last July," he said. "Three killed."

But that very morning in the south of France a slow-moving pilgrim train had slipped back from the top of a steep grade and telescoped itself on another train climbing the grade, making matchwood of two coaches and killing over thirty people. There had been a big falling off in business on the Paris-Strasbourg line after the July accident. But the same number of people seem to ride on railway trains.

The Franco-German Situation
The Toronto Daily Star, 14th April 1923

Paris. – To write about Germany you must begin by writing about France. There is a magic in the name France. It is a magic like the smell of the sea or the sight of blue hills or of soldiers marching by. It is a very old magic.

France is a broad and lovely country. The loveliest country that I know. It is impossible to write impartially about a country when you love it. But it is possible to write impartially about the government of that country. France refused in 1917 to make a peace without victory. Now she finds that she has a victory without peace. To understand why this is so we must take a look at the French government.

France at present is governed by a Chamber of Deputies elected in 1919. It was called the "horizon blue" parliament and is dominated by the famous "bloc national," or wartime coalition. This government has two more years to run.

The Liberals, who were the strongest group in France, were disgraced when Clemenceau destroyed their government in 1917 on the charge that they were negotiating for peace without victory from the Germans. Caillaux, admitted the best financier in France, the Liberal premier, was thrown into prison. There were almost-daily executions by firing squads of which no report appeared in the papers. Very many enemies of Clemenceau found themselves standing blindfolded against a stone wall at Versailles in the cold of the early morning while a young lieutenant nervously moistened his lips before he could give the command.

This Liberal group is practically unrepresented in the Chamber of Deputies. It is the great, unformed, unled opposition to the "bloc national" and it will be crystallized into form at the next election in 1924. You cannot live in France any length of time without having various people tell you in the strictest confidence that Caillaux will be prime minister again in 1924. If the occupation of the Ruhr fails he has a very good chance to be. There will be the inevitable reaction against the present government. The chance is that it will swing even further to the left and pass over Caillaux entirely to exalt Marcel Cachin, the Communist leader.

The present opposition to the "bloc national" in the Chamber of Deputies is furnished by the left. When you read of the right and the left in continental politics it refers to the way the members are seated in parliament. The conservatives are on the right, the monarchists are on the extreme right of the floor. The radicals are on the left. The Communists are on the extreme left. The extreme Communists are on the outside seats of the extreme left.

The French Communist party has 12 seats in the chamber out of 600. Marcel Cachin, editor of *L'Humanité*, with a circulation of 200,000, is the leader of the party. Vaillant Coutourier, a young subaltern of Chasseurs who was one of the most decorated men in France, is his lieutenant. The Communists led the opposition to M. Poincaré. They charge him with having brought on the war, with having desired the war; they always refer to him as "Poincaré la guerre." They charge him with being under the domination of Léon Daudet and the Royalists. They charge him with being under the domination of the iron kings, the coal kings; they charge him with many things, some of them very ridiculous.

M. Poincaré sits in the chamber with his little hands and little feet and his little white beard and when the Communists insult him too far, spits back at them like an angry cat. When it looks as though the Communists had uncovered any real dirt and members of the government begin to look doubtfully at M. Poincaré, Rene Viviani makes a speech. M. Viviani is the greatest orator of our times. You have only to hear M. Viviani pronounce the words "la gloire de France" to want to rush out and get into uniform. The next day after he has made his speech you find it posted up on posters all over the city.

Moscow has recently "purified" the French Communist party. According to the Russian Communists the French party was mawkishly patriotic and weak-willed. All members who refused to place themselves directly under orders from the central party in Moscow were asked to turn in their membership cards. A number did. The rest are now considered purified. But I doubt if they remain for long. The Frenchman is not a good internationalist.

The "bloc national" is made up of honest patriots, and representatives of the great steel trust, the coal trust, the wine industry, other smaller profiteers, ex-army officers, professional politicians, careerists, and the Royalists.

While it may seem fantastic to think of France having a king again, the Royalist party is extremely well organized, is very strong in certain parts of the south of France, controls several newspapers, including *L'Action Française*, and has organized a sort of Fascisti called the Camelots du Roi. It has a hand in everything in the government and was the greatest advocate of the advance into the Ruhr and the further occupation of Germany.

There, briefly, are the political parties in France and the way they line up. Now we must see the causes that forced France into the Ruhr.

France has spent eighty billion francs on reparations. Forty-five billion francs have been spent on reconstructing the devastated regions. There is a very great scandal talked in France about how that forty-five billions were spent. Deputy Inghies of the Department of the Nord, said the other day in the Chamber of Deputies that twenty-five billions of it went for graft. He offered to present the facts at any time the chamber would consent to hear him. He was hushed up. At any rate forty-five billions were spent wildly and rapidly and there are very many new "devastated region millionaires" in the Chamber of Deputies. The deputies asked for as much money as they wanted for their own districts and got it and a good part of the regions are still devastated.

The point is that the eighty billions have been spent and are charged up as collectible from Germany. They stand on the credit side of the ledger.

If at any time the French government admits that any part of those eighty billion francs are not collectible they must be moved over to the bad side of the ledger and listed as a loss rather than an asset. There are only thirty billions of paper francs in circulation today. If France admits that any part of the money spent and charged to Germany is uncollectible she must issue paper francs to pay the bonds she floated to raise the money she has spent. That means inflation in her currency, resulting in starting the franc on the greased skids the Austrian kronen and German mark traveled down.

When Aristide Briand, former prime minister, who looks like a bandit, and is the natural son of a French dancer and a café keeper of St. Nazaire, agreed at the Cannes Conference to a reduction in reparations in return for Lloyd George's defense pact, his ministry was overthrown almost before he could catch the train back to Paris. The weasel-eyed M. Arago, leader of the "bloc national," and Monsieur Barthou, who looks like the left-hand Smith Brother, were at Cannes watching every move of Briand and when they saw he was leaning toward a reduction of reparations they prepared to skid him out and get Poincaré in – and accomplished the coup before Briand knew what was happening to him. The "bloc national" cannot afford to have anyone cutting down on reparations because it does not want any inquiry as to how the money was spent. The memory of the Panama Canal scandal is still fresh.

Poincaré came into office and pledged to collect every sou possible from Germany. The story of how he was led to refuse the offer of the German industrialists to take over the payment of reparations if it was reduced to a reasonable figure, and the sinister tale that is unfolding day by day in the French Chamber of Deputies about how Poincaré was forced into the Ruhr against his own will and judgement, the strange story of the rise of Royalists in France and their influence on the present government will be told in the next article.

French Royalist Party
The Toronto Daily Star, 18th April 1923

Paris. – Raymond Poincaré is a changed man. Until a few months ago the little white-bearded Lorraine lawyer in his patent-leather shoes and his gray gloves dominated the French Chamber of Deputies with his methodical accountant's mind and his spitfire temper. Now he sits quietly and forlornly while fat, white-faced Léon Daudet shakes his finger at him and says "France will do this, France will do that."

Léon Daudet, son of old Alphonse Daudet, the novelist, is the leader of the Royalist party. He is also editor of *L'Action Française*, the Royalist paper, and author of *L'Entremetteuse*, or *The Procuress*, a novel whose plot could not even be outlined in any newspaper printed in English.

The Royalist party is perhaps the most solidly organized in France today. That is a surprising statement to those who think of France as a republic with no thought of ever being anything else. The Royalist headquarters are in Nîmes in the south of France and Provence is almost solidly Royalist. The Royalists have the solid support of the Catholic church. It being an easily understood fact that the church of Rome thrives better under European monarchies than under the French republic.

Philippe, the Duke of Orleans, is the Royalist's candidate for king. Philippe lives in England, is a big, good-looking man and rides very well to hounds. He is not allowed by law to enter France.

There is a Royalist Fascisti called the Camelots du Roi. They carry black loaded canes with salmon-colored handles and at twilight you can see them in Montmartre swaggering along the streets with their canes, a little way ahead and behind a news-boy who is crying *L'Action Française* in the radical quarter of the old Butte. Newsboys who carry *L'Action Française* into radical districts without the protecting guard of Camelots are badly beaten up by the Communists and Socialists.

In the past year the Royalists have received a tremendous impetus in some mysterious way. It has come on so rapidly and suddenly that from being more or less of a joke they are now spoken of as one of the very strongest parties. In fact Daudet is marked for assassination by the extreme radicals and men are not assassinated until they are considered dangerous. An attempt on his life was made by an anarchist a month or so ago. The girl assassin killed his assistant, Marius Plateau, by mistake.

General [Charles] Mangin, the famous commander of attack troops, nicknamed "The Butcher," is a Royalist. He was the only great French general who was not made a marshal. He can always be seen in the Chamber of Deputies when Léon Daudet is to speak. It is the only time he comes.

Now the Royalist party wants no reparations from Germany. Nothing would frighten them more than if Germany should be able to pay in full tomorrow. For that would mean that Germany was becoming strong. What they want is a weak Germany, dismembered if possible, a return to the military glories and conquests of France, the return of the Catholic church, and the return of the king. But being patriotic as all Frenchmen, they first want to obtain security by weakening Germany permanently. Their plan to accomplish this is to have the reparations kept at such a figure that will be unpayable and then seize German territory to be held "only until reparations are paid."

The very sinister mystery is how they obtained the hold over M. Poincaré to force him to fall in with their plan and refuse to even discuss the German industrialists' proposal to take over the payment of reparations if they were reduced to a reasonable figure. The German industrialists have money, have been making money ever since the armistice, have profited by the fall of the mark to sell in pounds and dollars and pay their workers in worthless marks, and have most of their pounds and dollars salted away. But they did not have enough money to pay the reparations as they were listed, and they wanted to make some sort of a final settlement with the French.

Now, we must get back to the little white-whiskered Raymond Poincaré, who has the smallest hands and feet of any man I have ever seen, sitting in the chair at the Chamber of Deputies, while the fat, white-faced Léon Daudet, who wrote the obscene novel and leads the Royalists and is marked for assassination, shakes his finger at him and says, "France will do this, France will do that."

To understand what is going on we must remember that French politics is unlike any other. It is a very intimate politics, a politics of scandal. Remember the duels of Clemenceau, the Calmette killing, the figure of the last president of the French republic [Deschanel] standing in a fountain at the Bois and saying: "Oh, don't let them get me. Don't let them get me."

A few days ago M. André Berthon stood up in the Chamber of Deputies and said: "Poincaré, you are the prisoner of Léon Daudet. I demand to know by what blackmail he holds you. I do not understand why the government of M. Poincaré submits to the dictatorship of Léon Daudet, the Royalist."

"Tout d'une pièce," all in one piece, as the *Matin* described it, Poincaré jumped up and said: "You are an abominable *gredin*, Monsieur." Now you cannot call a man anything worse than a *gredin*, although it means nothing particularly bad in English. The chamber rocked with shouts and catcalls. It looked like the free fight in the cigarette factory when Geraldine Farrar first began to play Carmen. Finally it quieted down sufficiently for M. Poincaré, trembling and gray with rage, to say: "The man who stands in the Tribune dares to say that there exist against me or mine abominable dossiers which I fear to have made public. I deny it."

M. Berthon said very sweetly: "I have not mentioned any dossiers." Dossiers are literally bundles of papers. It is the technical name for the French system of keeping all the documents on the case in a big manila folder. To have a dossier against you is to have all the official papers proving a charge held by someone with the power to use them.

In the end M. Berthon was asked to apologize. "I apologize for any outrageous words I may have used." He did so very sweetly. It took this form: "I only say, Monsieur le Président, that Monsieur Léon Daudet exercises a sort of pressure on your politics."

This apology was accepted. Poincaré, goaded out of his depression to deny the existence of papers that had not been mentioned, is back in his forlornness. You cannot make charges in France unless you hold the papers in your hands and those that do hold dossiers know how to use them.

Last July in a confidential conversation with a number of British and American newspaper correspondents Poincaré, discussing the Ruhr situation, said: "Occupation would be futile and absurd. Obviously Germany can only pay now in goods and labor." He was a more cheerful Poincaré in those days.

Meantime the French government has spent 160 million francs (official) on the occupation and Ruhr coal is costing France $200 a ton.

Government Pays for News
The Toronto Daily Star, 21st April 1923

Paris. – What do the French people think about the Ruhr and the whole German question? You will not find out by reading the French press.

French newspapers sell their news columns just as they do their advertising space. It is quite open and understood. As a matter of fact it is not considered very chic to advertise in the small advertising section of a French daily. The news item is supposed to be the only real way of advertising.

So the government pays the newspapers a certain amount to print government news. It is considered government advertising and every big French daily like *Le Matin*, *Petit Parisien*, *Echo de Paris*, *L'Intransigeant*, *Le Temps* receives a regular amount in subsidy for printing government news. Thus the government is the newspapers' biggest advertising client. But that is all the news on anything the government is doing that the readers of the paper get.

When the government has any special news, as it has at such a time as the occupation of the Ruhr, it pays the papers extra. If any of these enormously circulated daily papers refuse to print the government news or criticize the government standpoint, the government withdraws its subsidy – and the paper loses its biggest advertiser. Consequently the big Paris dailies are always for the government, any government that happens to be in.

When one of them refuses to print the news furnished by the government and begins attacking its policy you may be sure of one thing. That it has not accepted the loss of its subsidy without receiving the promise of a new one and a substantial advance from some government that it is absolutely sure will get into power shortly. And it has to be awfully sure it is coming off before it turns down its greatest client. Consequently when one of these papers whose circulation mounts into millions starts an attack on the government it is time for the politicians in power to get out their overshoes and put up the storm windows.

All of these things are well-known and accepted facts. The government's attitude is that the newspapers are not in business for their health and that they must pay for the news they get like any other advertiser. The newspapers have confirmed the government in this attitude.

Le Temps is always spoken of as "semi-official." That means that the first column on the front page is written in the foreign office at the Quai d'Orsay, the rest of the columns are at the disposal of the various governments of Europe. A sliding scale of rates handles them. Unimportant governments can get space cheap. Big governments come high. All European governments have a special fund for newspaper publicity that does not have to be accounted for.

This sometimes leads to amusing incidents as a year ago, when the facts were published showing how *Le Temps* was receiving subsidies for running propaganda for two different Balkan governments who were at loggerheads and printing the dispatches as their own special correspondence on alternate days. No matter how idealistic European politics may be, a trusting idealist is about as safe in its machinery as a blind man stumbling about in a sawmill. One of my best friends was in charge of getting British propaganda printed in the Paris press at the close of the war. He is as sincere and idealistic a man as one could know – but he certainly knows where the buzz saws are located and how the furnace is stoked.

In spite of the fact that the great Paris dailies, which are so widely quoted in the States and Canada as organs of public opinion, say that the people of France are solidly backing the occupation of the Ruhr, it is nevertheless true. France always backs the government in anything it does against a foreign foe once the government has started. It is that really wonderful patriotism of the French. All Frenchmen are patriotic – and nearly all Frenchmen are politicians. But the absolute backing of the government only lasts a certain length of time. Then after the white heat has cooled, the Frenchman looks the situation over, the facts begin to circulate around, he discovers that the occupation is not a success – and overthrows the government. The Frenchman feels he must be absolutely loyal to his government but he can overthrow it and get a new government to be loyal to at any time.

Marshal Foch, for example, was opposed to the Ruhr occupation. He washed his hands of it absolutely. But once it was launched, he did not come out against it. He sent General [Maxime] Weygand, his chief of staff, to oversee it and do the best he could. But he does not want to be associated with it in any way.

Similarly Loucheur, the former minister of the liberated regions, and one of the ablest men in France, opposed the occupation. Loucheur is a man who does not mince words. During the period when France was pouring out money for reconstruction with seemingly no regard as to how it was spent or for what, Loucheur did all he could to control it. It was Loucheur who told the mayor of Rheims: "Monsieur, you are asking exactly six times the cost of this reconstruction."

A few days ago M. Loucheur said to me in conversation, "I was always opposed to the occupation. It is impossible to get any money that way. But now that they have gone in, now that the flag of France is unfurled, we are all Frenchmen and we must loyally support the occupation."

M. André Tardieu, who headed the French mission to the United States during the war and is Clemenceau's lieutenant, opposed the advance into the Ruhr in his paper, the *Echo National*, up until the day it started. Now he is denouncing it as ill-run, badly managed, wishy-washy and not strong enough. M. Tardieu, who looks like a bookmaker, foresees the failure of the present government with the failure of the occupation but he wants to be in a position to catch the reaction in the bud and say: "Give us a chance at it. Let us show that, properly handled, it can be a success." For M. Tardieu is a very astute politician and that is very nearly his only chance of getting back into power for some time.

Edouard Herriot, mayor of Lyons, a member of the cabinet during the war, and dark-horse candidate for next premier of France, after supporting the occupation in the same way that Loucheur is doing, has now sponsored a resolution in the Lyons city council protesting the occupation and demanding consideration of a financial and economic entente with Germany. This demand of Herriot may be the first puff of the wind that is bound to rise and blow the Poincaré government out of power.

Now why are these, and many other intelligent Frenchmen, opposed to the occupation although they want to get every cent possible from Germany? It is simply because of the way it is going. It is losing France money instead of making it and from the start it was seen by the long-headed financiers that it would only cripple Germany's ability to pay further reparations, unite her as a country and reflame her hatred against France – and cost more money than it would ever get out.

Before the occupation a train of twelve or more cars of coal or coke left the Ruhr for France every twenty-eight minutes. Now there are only two trains a day. A train of twelve cars is now split up into four trains to pad the figures and make the occupation look successful.

When there is a shipment of coal to be gotten out, four or five tanks, a battalion of infantry, and fifty workmen go to do the job. The soldiers are to prevent the inhabitants beating up the workmen. The official figures on the amount of coal and coke that has been exported from the Ruhr and the money that has already been given by the Chamber of Deputies for the first months of the occupation show that the coal France was receiving as her reparations account is now costing her a little over $200 a ton. And she isn't getting the coal.

At the start of the occupation certain correspondents wrote that it would be easy for France to run the Ruhr profitably, all she would have to do would be to bring in cheap labor – Italian or Polish labor is always cheap – and just get the stuff out. The other day I saw some of this cheap labor locked in a car at the Gare du Nord bound for Essen. They were a miserable lot of grimy unfit-looking men, the sort that could not get work in France, or anywhere else. They were all drunk, some shouting, some asleep on the floor of the car, some sick. They looked more like a shanghaied ship's crew than anything else. And they were all going to be paid double wages and work halftime under military protection. No workmen will go into the Ruhr for less than double wages – and it has been almost impossible to get workmen for that. The Poles and Italians will not touch the job. If you want any further information on the way it works out economically, ask any businessman or any street railway head who has ever had a strike how much money his corporation made during the time it was employing strikebreakers.

Now that we have seen in a quick glance the forces that are at work in France in this war after the war, the situation of France, and the views of her people, we can next look at Germany.

Gargoyles as Symbol
The Toronto Star Weekly, 17th November 1923

It would be difficult to find a detail of architecture that is more popular with the European tourists than the gargoyles of Notre Dame in Paris. Thousands have climbed the weary stone stairs to examine them in detail and then examine, from above, the magnificent panorama of the French capital. But the gargoyles are pleasant fellows to meet, with their grinning faces and elfish profiles; all pleasant but two. And those two are located on the northeastern aspect of the tower that looks out toward Germany. These two are the hungry gargoyles. The one is swallowing a long, luckless dog, while its companion gazes greedily down toward the land where France is now encamped.

But, the tourists will remonstrate, Notre Dame was built centuries ago. How could the present-day attitude of France be veiled in their horrible visage?

Truly the cathedral was built more than six hundred years ago, but these gargoyles were executed and placed in position there by order of Napoleon the Third, a short time before the outbreak of the Franco-Prussian war. The cathedral is old; but these monstrosities are not. They belong to modern history and the commencement of French hatred toward the eastern neighbor.

These world-famed gargoyles were placed on Notre Dame by E.E. Viollet-le-Duc, who died in 1879. He was an intimate friend of Napoleon the Third, and was employed in the restoration of many ancient buildings that had suffered during the French Revolution. In that connection he was engaged with his Notre Dame gargoyles for eleven years. Other buildings which he restored with figures do not exhibit the horror and rapacity of these two gargoyles which face Germany. Did he here express, in stone, the thoughts of the French leaders which are now current history?

European Nightlife: A Disease
The Toronto Star Weekly, 15th December 1923

Nightlife in Europe is not simply a list of cafés. It is a sort of strange disease, always existent, that has been fanned into flame since the war. Its flame is burning an entire generation.

Paris nightlife is the most highly civilized and amusing. Berlin is the most sordid, desperate and vicious. Madrid is the dullest, and Constantinople is, or was, the most exciting.

Paris goes to bed the earliest of any big town in the world. Promptly at twelve-thirty o'clock the last omnibuses leave on their crosstown trips, the last subway train roars along the Metro, and the streets around the Opéra empty as though a curfew had sounded. Taxis leave the streets to drive home, and the final trains are jammed with Parisians on their way home.

Paris is dead. Hours before, shutters have been up and the residential quarters tight asleep. There remain only the night-hawks. Where do thy go?

There are three oases of light in the tight-shuttered darkness of a Paris night.

One of them is Montparnasse. Here the Latin Quarter cafés keep open a couple of hours more. There is no place in the world deader than a Montparnasse café unless you know the crowd. If you know the people, it is a club and a center for gossip, a common meeting place.

Where is the really gay Paris nightlife we hear so much about? Where are the young people who never go to bed at night? The people that do not exist before ten o'clock at night?

They are probably packed into a little place around the corner from the Hôtel Crillon in the staidest, most respectable, un-Bohemian quarter of Paris. In the Rue Boissy d'Anglais is the café of the Boeuf sur le Toit or the Bull-on-the-Roof, Jean Cocteau's bar and dancing, where everyone in Paris who believes that the true way to burn the candle is by igniting it at both ends goes. By eleven o'clock the Boeuf is so crowded that there is no more room to dance. But all the world is there. Sitting at tables, talking and drinking while the jazz plays.

But French nightlife is so civilized that it is not exciting to the outsider. Nightlife is a sort of state of mind. Either you are in it or you are out of it. It is in Cocteau's bar that nightlife in the highest sense – that of living at night – is brought to the boiling point.

The Boeuf, though, closes at two in the morning. Sometimes before. And two in the morning is when the true nightlifer is just getting under way. So in a taxi the nightlifer starts up the slopes of Montparnasse.

Montmartre is the famous Paris place for night activity. It is compounded of the garish tourist traps around the Place de

Clichy, with red-painted doors and thousands of electric light globes. These have fantastic names and fake artists who are hired to come in and sit at the tables to give a Bohemian atmosphere. They are run for the purpose of getting Americans, both North and South, to buy champagne.

Champagne is the great symbol of nightlife to the uninitiated. And the tourist traps make the most of it. They sell champagne and champagne only. If the visitor tries to order anything else, he is given the choice of champagne or the street door. It ranges in price from six to eight dollars a bottle. While it is being drunk, the tourist can look around at other tourists and the hired artists who are dressed in Greenwich Village costumes.

Champagne, by the way, is a sacred name in France. The only wine allowed by law to be called champagne wine comes from a certain defined district around Rheims in the Champagne province. Other fake champagne must be labeled Epernay, mousseux or whatever district they come from. There is a terrific fine for selling these wines from just outside the champagne district as the veritable wine. The real champagne vintners have important government connections.

A patriotic-minded journalist heard that a certain Montmartre resort was selling mousseux as champagne. With a witness, he went into the place and ordered a single glass of champagne. He was served a sparkling liquid, the bubbles hopping and jumping to the surface. He paid a champagne price. The waiter went away.

The journalist tasted the glass. "Mousseux!" he shouted. "The camel has served me with mousseux and I ordered champagne. What an outrage. Not only an outrage, but a breaking of the law. Bring the proprietor. Bring the proprietor instantly before I send for the police."

The proprietor is reported to have settled the case for 20,000 francs.

Numberless other journalists and men-about-town ordered glasses of champagne after that, hoping for such a chance, but the mousseux sellers were wise. It was not worth the chance. It is costly business mistaking a Frenchman for a tourist.

The famous Moulin Rouge on Montmartre is an enormous dancing place where shop girls, their gentlemen friends, and a certain number of tourists go to dance on a large and slippery floor in the glare cast by a spotlight that is supposed to give romance through different-colored celluloid disks that make a red, orange, or green glow. It is cheerful and innocuous, and one of the few places in Paris where the foreigners come into contact with French people taking their pleasure.

The real nightlife places do not open up until after three o'clock in the morning. At present the two most notable of these are the Caucasian, a very smart Russian place, and Florence's. Florence is an American Negress who has made a tremendous vogue for herself in Paris as a dancer.

When I first met her some time ago, she was a typical Negro dancer, jolly, funny and wonderful on her feet. Until you had seen Florence dance the "Everybody Steps," you had seen nothing.

Then a section of the French nobility took her up. She danced at the home of the Princesse de This and the Comtesse de That. Late last summer we wandered into Florence's dancing place to get some corn-beef hash with poached egg and buckwheat cakes at two-thirty in the morning. It was absolutely dead. No one had come in yet. The Negro staff were not overeager to serve us. They thought we ought to buy champagne.

Now the mark of a real student of nightlife is that he should be considered so much of an asset to a place that the compulsory-consumption-of-champagne rule should be suspended in his favor.

"We're old friends of Florence," I explained.

"Suah, boss. What'll you all have? Beeah? Anythin' you say, boss."

We had a good meal, and then Florence came in. Florence was changed. She had acquired an English accent and a languid manner.

"Oh. Hulloa," she said. "Yes, I'm dawncing private now. But do drop in on us sometime heah. So jolly to see you again."

It wasn't jolly at all. Another of the really amusing after-midnight places had been ruined by prosperity.

"Miss Flawnce she ain't a Niggah no mo. No suh. She done tell customahs mammy's an Indian lady fum Canada," a waiter explained. "Ah'm luhnin' to talk that English way, too. Ah'm goin' tuh tell people my mammy's an Indian lady fuhm Noble Scotia. Yes, suh. We'll all be Indiums this tahm nex' yeah. Yes, suh."

There are other famous nocturnal places in Paris – Zelli's, where the newspapermen all used to go, the very dressy dancings in the Rue Caumartin, where one would find Peggy Joyce and other famous ladies of the front page, and sleek-haired Chileans and Argentineans dancing to American jazz music.

Berlin's nightlife is a great contrast to that of Paris. Berlin is a vulgar, ugly, sullenly dissipated city. After the war it plunged into an orgy that the Germans called the death dance. There is nothing attractive nor gay about the nightlife of Berlin. It is altogether revolting.

If champagne is the deus ex machin of the after-hours existence of Paris, cocaine takes its place in the German capital. Cocaine peddlers get short shrift from the Paris police. But in Berlin they sell their wares openly all over the city. In some cafés cocaine is served at the tables by the waiters.

Berlin is the home of the nightclub. Riding or walking along the street at night, a ragged-looking man will run up to your cab and try to get you to go to a nightclub. A fine new nightclub. All the nightlife of the city.

There is no nightclub in Berlin that is not disgusting, heavy, dull and hopeless. The gaiety is as forced as it is real in Paris on the 14th of July, when the entire city dances in the street for two nights steady and the streets are roped off to shut out taxis and autobuses.

If anyone had any doubt that the Germans lost the war and realize they lost it, all they need would be a session of after-midnight Berlin.

Madrid is another business. Nobody goes to bed in Madrid. On the other hand, they don't do anything to amuse themselves. They just stay up and talk.

All of the downtown district of Madrid is at its very busiest at two o'clock in the morning. Cafés are crowded. The streets are jammed with people. Theaters start in Madrid at ten o'clock at night. Matinees commence at 6:30 in the afternoon.

There are two big downtown dancing places. One called Maxim's. The other, two or three doors up the street, I have forgotten the name of. It makes no difference. They are both alike.

Always beware of a place called Maxim's. It means imitation Paris. Now Paris is a fine thing. But it doesn't imitate well. And there are Maxim's all over the world.

Even the original Maxim's in Paris is a dull enough place. It has a bar as you go in and then a big room full of tables, with a dancing floor at the far end. It is always full of profiteers, American buyers, and the inevitable sprinkling of South Americans. The music plays loudly and the prices are high. The lights are bright. It is a good place to get a headache.

All the imitation Maxim's are reproductions on a small scale of the original.

In Madrid I asked a bullfighter where the really gay life of the city was. Where he went himself, for example.

"Me? I go to bed," he smiled shyly. "I don't like to talk and I don't like to drink. Since I have learned to read, I read a little every night in bed before I go to sleep."

"What do you read?" I asked.

"Oh, the bullfighting papers," he said.

He is a very serious young man, makes $15,000 a year, and probably has half the girls in Madrid in love with him. But he doesn't believe in nightlife.

Constantinople before the Mudania armistice was probably the most hectic town in the world. Mustapha Kemal had announced that when he came into town it was going to be shut tight up – and everybody believed him. He had done everything he ever said he would up till then.

Nobody slept much during the day and nobody slept at all during the night. No good restaurants opened up before ten at night and the theaters opened at midnight. The followers of the prophet spent their waking hours trying to make absolutely sure there would be none of the product of Constantinople's Bavarian breweries left to dump into the Golden Horn when Kemal arrived.

The breweries tried to keep pace with the Moslem demand. It was a great race. Along toward evening, the crews of the British, American, Spanish, Italian and French fleets would come ashore and rush to the aid of the Mohammedans in their struggle with the breweries. It was a great battle, with the brewers always a little ahead. In spite of their smaller numbers, their organization was better.

As the evening advanced fights would break out among the sailors of the different nationalities in the various Galata beer emporiums. This no doubt slowed up their efficiency. Especially when there were shootings or knifings, which occasionally resulted in pitched battles.

All of Constantinople was in a feverish sort of wildness. It had nothing of the sullen ugliness of the Berlin pleasure resorts.

There is the famous incident of the captain of a cruiser of a neutral nation, not the United States, whose vessel was anchored in the Bosporus. The incident came very near to being of tremendous international gravity.

One night at three o'clock in the morning, the commander came aboard his ship. His manner was distrait. His eyes were rolling.

"Clear the ship for action," he commanded.

The commander paced restlessly up and down the bridge. The ship was as busy as only a warship with its crew suddenly roused at three a.m. can be. Men rushed in every direction. Guns were trained for a broadside.

"Commence firing on the city," the captain shouted down his telephone from the bridge. "War has been declared."

Somebody had sense enough to grab him and take him below. Constantinople had been a little too much for him.

The captain was said to have been drinking douzico straight. It has a faculty of making people go crazy at odd times. It is prepared with some sort of strange Turkish ingredients, but its base is grain alcohol imported from the United States in large steel drums. It was never served without some crackers, cheese or radishes to give it something to work on in addition to the lining of the stomach.

From Stamboul across the Golden Horn to the high barren plain at the top of Pera, Constan stayed up all night. Every big newspaper story that broke came after midnight in the night-clubs of Pera. It was in one of these, the Pele Mele, in some way derived from Pall Mall, that an excited young officer just back on a destroyer from Mudania confided the news of the signing of the armistice to a Russian countess who was acting as a waitress.

The officer, who had been present at the signing, told the countess in greatest secrecy because he had to tell someone. He was so excited. She recognized the value of the story and told an American newspaperman whom she liked much better than she did the officer.

In an hour, through means of his own, the newspaperman verified the report, and put it on the cable to New York, where it arrived in time for the morning papers. The signing was not announced officially until next morning at eleven o'clock. By that time the correspondents of the other papers, whose correspondents did not know the countess, were getting cables from New York asking them why they were scooped on Mudania.

Italy is a strange country for nightlife. Nightlife must be taken to mean, not dissipation or dancing places necessarily, but merely that strange, feverish something that keeps people up and about during the hours they would normally sleep.

Milan, the largest city in the north of Italy, with about 800,000 inhabitants, goes to bed almost as early as Toronto does. Verona, not a third as big, is alive and gay at two-thirty in the morning. I remember hiking into Verona with a pack long after midnight expecting to find everything closed tight, and finding the city as alive as Paris at 9:30 in the evening.

Turin is another late town, and a very pleasant town. Rome is very dull at night. Rome, to my mind, is very dull nearly all of the time. It is the last city in the world I would ever want to live in.

Marseilles has one of the most variegated, interesting and toughest night sides in Europe.

Seville, too, is late to bed. So is Granada.

Nightlife is a funny thing. There seems to be no reason or rule that controls it. You cannot find it when you want it. And you cannot get away from it when you don't want it. It is a European product.

Christmas in Paris
The Toronto Star Weekly, 22nd December 1923

Paris with the snow falling. Paris with the big charcoal braziers outside the cafés, glowing red. At the café tables, men huddled, their coat collars turned up, while they finger glasses of grog *Americain* and the newsboys shout the evening papers.

The buses rumble like green juggernauts through the snow that sifts down in the dusk. White house walls rise through the dusky snow. Snow is never more beautiful than in the city. It is wonderful in Paris to stand on a bridge across the Seine looking up through the softly curtaining snow past the gray bulk of the Louvre, up the river spanned by many bridges and bordered by the gray houses of old Paris to where Notre Dame squats in the dusk.

It is very beautiful in Paris and very lonely at Christmastime.

The young man and his girl walk up the Rue Bonaparte from the Quai in the shadow of the tall houses to the brightly lighted little Rue Jacob. In a little second-floor restaurant, The Veritable Restaurant of the Third Republic, which has two rooms, four tiny tables and a cat, there is a special Christmas dinner being served.

"It isn't much like Christmas," said the girl.

"I miss the cranberries," said the young man.

They attack the special Christmas dinner. The turkey is cut into a peculiar sort of geometrical formation that seems to include a small taste of meat, a great deal of gristle, and a large piece of bone.

"Do you remember turkey at home?" asks the young girl.

"Don't talk about it," says the boy.

They attack the potatoes, which are fried with too much grease.

"What do you suppose they're doing at home?" says the girl.

"I don't know," said the boy. "Do you suppose we'll ever get home?"

"I don't know," the girl answered. "Do you suppose we'll ever be successful artists?"

The proprietor entered with the dessert and a small bottle of red wine.

"I had forgotten the wine," he said in French.

The girl began to cry.

"I didn't know Paris was like this," she said. "I thought it was gay and full of light and beautiful."

The boy put his arm around her. At least that was one thing you could do in a Parisian restaurant.

"Never mind, honey," he said. "We've been here only three days. Paris will be different. Just you wait."

They ate the dessert, and neither one mentioned the fact that it was slightly burned. Then they paid the bill and walked downstairs and out into the street. The snow was still falling. And they walked out into the streets of old Paris that had known the prowling of wolves and the hunting of men and the tall old houses that had looked down on it all and were stark and unmoved by Christmas.

The boy and the girl were homesick. It was their first Christmas away from their own land. You do not know what Christmas is until you lose it in some foreign land.

Biographical note

Ernest Hemingway did more to change the style of English prose than any other writer of his time. Publication of *The Sun Also Rises* and *A Farewell to Arms* immediately established him as one of the greatest literary lights of the twentieth century. As part of the expatriate community in 1920s Paris, the former journalist and World War I ambulance driver began a career that led to international fame. Hemingway was an aficionado of bullfighting and big-game hunting, and his main protagonists were always men and women of courage and conviction who suffered unseen scars, both physical and emotional. He covered the Spanish Civil War, portraying it in the novel *For Whom the Bell Tolls*, and he also covered World War II. His classic novella *The Old Man and the Sea* won the Pulitzer Prize in 1953. Hemingway was awarded the Nobel Price for Literature in 1954. He died in 1961.

Under our three imprints, Hesperus Press publishes over 300 books by many of the greatest figures in worldwide literary history, as well as sensational contemporary and debut authors well worth discovering.

Hesperus Classics handpicks the best of worldwide and translated literature, introducing forgotten and neglected books to new generations.

Hesperus Nova showcases quality contemporary fiction and non-fiction designed to entertain and inspire.

Hesperus Minor rediscovers well-loved children's books from the past – these are books which will bring back fond memories for adults, which they will want to share with their children and loved ones.

To find out more visit www.hesperuspress.com
@HesperusPress